FAT
NO MORE

A Teenager's Victory over Obesity

FAT NO MORE

A Teenager's Victory over Obesity

Alberto Hidalgo-Robert

PIÑATA
BOOKS

PIÑATA BOOKS
ARTE PÚBLICO PRESS
HOUSTON, TEXAS

Fat No More: A Teenager's Victory over Obesity is made possible through a grant from the City of Houston through the Houston Arts Alliance.

Piñata Books are full of surprises!

Arte Público Press
University of Houston
4902 Gulf Fwy, Bldg 19, Rm 100
Houston, Texas 77204-2004

Cover design by Mora Des!gn Group
All photos courtesy of Alberto Hidalgo-Robert

Hidalgo-Robert, Alberto
    Fat No More: A Teenager's Victory over Obesity / by Alberto Hidalgo-Robert
        p. cm.
    ISBN 978-1-55885-745-2 (alk. paper)
        1. Hidalgo-Robert, Alberto—Health. 2. Weight loss—Juvenile literature. 3. Eating disorders in adolescence—Juvenile literature. 4. Teenagers—Nutrition—Juvenile literature. I. Title.
    RM222.2.H44 2012
    616.85'2600835—dc23
                                                            2012003177
                                                                 CIP

Printed in the United States of America
April 2012–May 2012
United Graphics, Inc., Mattoon, IL
12 11 10 9 8 7 6 5 4 3 2 1

Table of Contents

Acknowledgements

I AM VERY INCREDIBLY GRATEFUL TO EVERYONE WHO MADE *Fat No More: A Teenager's Victory over Obesity* possible and who encouraged, inspired and supported me during and after my transformation. First and foremost, I would like to thank my fans and readers, for taking a chance with me and my book. You all inspired me to put my story out there.

I also would like to thank my parents, Cecilia and Hugo Hidalgo—I love you, unconditionally, with all my heart. You guys are my rock. Furthermore, I would like to thank my family and my old and new friends. I love you all and thank God, every single day, for having you in my life.

I also want to thank my literary agent Leticia Gomez, for taking a chance with me. Arte Público Press and Nicolás Kanellos, for giving me the opportunity of a life time. My editing partners Pamela Guerrieri and Kimberly Jayce. My fairy godparents Cindy Zedeck, Dr. Thomas Robinson and the Weight Control Program at Lucile Packard Children's Hospital. I'm forever grateful for all the amazing things you have done for me. My humble appreciation is indescribable.

You yourself, as much as anybody in the entire universe, deserve your love and affection.

—Gautama Buddha

Foreword

Obesity's Chestnut

What is this? Who am I? Why in the world did I write this book?

MY STORY STARTS WITH A FIVE-YEAR-OLD KID HOLDING A LARGE chocolate milkshake and an extra-large order of french fries. *What's wrong with this picture?*

Well, first thing, it looked like the milkshake weighed more than the kid holding it. He almost dropped the cup as soon as it was placed in his tiny hands.

Let's be realistic! We live in the twenty-first century in the most "supersized" country of them all. So let's face reality here. Let's not lie to ourselves—because you, your mom and dad, your brothers and sisters, your dogs, your cat and your canary know that, nowadays, a ten-pound milkshake is considered "normal."

But realistically, what *is* normal when it comes to food? Two plus two equals four; that's normal. Going to school is normal. Breathing is normal. Eating is normal. But E.T. (remember him?) is not normal, and the day I saw that child was just like an E.T. experience for me. A five-year-old kid about to drink a milkshake he could barely hold up is crazy—it's out of this world!

What is wrong with us?

Did I mention that the milkshake was bigger than the kid's head? Tip: Anything bigger than your head should not be eaten by anyone—not by and especially not by a five-year-old child.

When someone who weighs barely fifty pounds is about to drink—from one glass—something that weighs up to five percent of his weight, that is not normal.

And really, did he need the extra-large fries? Does a fifty-pound child need an extra-large serving of anything?

All this begs the question: Where were the parents? By buying that food for him, they were giving their approval to unhealthy food choices. They didn't need their voice boxes to do so. They were letting their child fall prey to something called manipulation, and also something that they might consider to be unconditional love.

In the first chapter of this book, you'll discover how those two factors can affect a child from the day he is born through the rest of his days.

But how does this E.T. episode relate to my memoir?

Fourteen years ago, I *was* that kid with the large chocolate milkshake in one hand and the extra-large order of french fries in the other. How did I end up? Like a limping dog—in pain, deprived of self-esteem and self-confidence, with an enormous lack of self-respect, completely alienated from self-love. You'll see.

Just as an appetizer, let me tell you a fact about me and my journey: I ended up weighing as much as a newborn baby elephant! And if that kid I saw holding the overgrown milkshake keeps eating that way—if the kid's parents let him keep eating that way—then he'll end up on the route I was traveling on. I'm not talking about the road less traveled, folks, but rather the one that a good 60 percent of our nation is now traveling.

My name is Alberto Hidalgo-Robert or—as my friends Rukshana, Megan and Miriam call me—Bert, for short. And because I'm your friend now, and because you became part of this crazy, circus-like ride the moment you picked up this book, you are welcome to call me that too!

I was born in the tiniest country in Central America, little bean-shaped El Salvador, on September 12, 1991. I was the first son, grandson, nephew and great-grandson of a tiny family: ten people maximum. In November 2002, my parents and I immigrated to Redwood City, California, where we now reside—and where we remain a tiny family.

By trade, I'm a college student at Notre Dame de Namur University, where I study biochemistry. I'm also the founder of an online anti-obesity campaign, *Healthy Bert: No Child Left with a Big Behind Foundation*. You might have read one of my blogs, or you may have seen one of my YouTube videos, or you might follow me on Twitter . . . or maybe, just maybe, you've cooked one of my healthy recipes.

For those who don't know me, I want to welcome you to my zany journey and life. Hello, friend I haven't met yet! No matter what you already know about me, what you do *not* know about me is what I want to share with you in the following pages.

Have you noticed how the problem of obesity has grown nonstop in this country in the past few years? I used to be part of that cadre of obese Americans. Not long ago, my life was about to crumble down . . . and it would have, if it hadn't been for the Lucile Packard Weight Control Program, the healthy "tools" I was presented with and my parents (keep reading, and you'll understand how everything came into play).

Being so close to losing that battle was the worst feeling I've ever experienced. It was as if I were signing my life over to the devil. I felt like I was trying to fight a battle unarmed, without a scintilla of self-love. Self-love is described by the *World English Dictionary* as "the instinct or tendency to seek one's own well-being or to further one's own interests." The container where my self-love was supposed to be was unoccupied. Vacant. Empty. I had zero, nil, nada.

What I didn't have in self-respect, I had in weight: more than sixty pounds of excess weight and about to cross into the Diabetic Zone. I went *that* far! I almost ended up giving up my life, dreams and hopes, handing them over to Obesity. I don't want you to go through what I went through. I'd rather make my life an obese example *not* to follow. I'd rather let my story be known than hear that the statistics of kids dying due to the effects of obesity are increasing by the hour. I'd rather you laugh at my crazy experiences and episodes, and learn something from them. I'd rather share my Tools, in every single chapter, than see *you* heading for the thin ice. I'd rather help you than waste the knowledge I've learned. Becoming your health template would be more rewarding than keeping this knowledge to myself and seeing you deteriorate, bit by bit. I'd rather use that knowledge to help you save your life or help you help others save their lives.

Oh yeah! I forgot to tell you. Once you finish this book, you will have many weapons to counteract obesity and build a healthier life—and I don't want you to waste those weapons. I want this to be a domino effect. I'll give you information, you give information to someone else and they pass it along and so on. Why waste useful weapons and let our lives go to waste? So this book is not only about you learning; it is about you learning and then becoming the teacher. You'll be like a health guru!

Last-minute words:

I know I am not the greatest philosopher or novelist of all time, but I'm a young adult who has taken the responsibility to help others save their own lives and other people's lives. I'm a young adult who has taken the responsibility to promote a healthy lifestyle. I have taken the responsibility to protect others from Obesity.

My writing is probably not the best; sometimes I won't make sense. I know that if I've made a thousand grammar mistakes or have used the wrong wording too often, I might lose you. But if, because of my journey, you absorb at least one new healthy habit—either an eating or an exercising habit—I will know my hard work is paying off and your new life has become a work in progress.

Revolutionizing your life and turning it into a healthier life takes time. You might get frustrated, tired, annoyed or mad, but let me tell you something: Do not give up! Also, remember that now you have a new friend, *me*, who will take you by the hand. You can take my crazy, hilarious stories with you wherever you want, and I'll be right next to you. With this book, you can let me lead you to a healthier lifestyle, by sharing my journey. I'll be here 24/7.

Pretend my "fable," if you want to call it that, is like a lunch menu. First of all, you will have to sit and relax; breathe in, breathe out.

Then we will start with an appetizer—which, in this case, will be the stories behind my bulging fat, the history of my limping life and stretch marks. After finishing my appetizer, we will dive right into the main dish, which will contain all the secrets behind how I won the battle. You'll learn the truth behind the pounds I lost. In other words, the main dish will be like the juicy, delicious, grilled patty in a hamburger—the best part!

At last, we will get to the dessert (the second-best part!) In this memoir, the dessert will represent the end of my struggle against my demon and the beginning of my new life. It will include the beginning of my self-love, the beginning of my ability to walk down the street without looking straight down at the gray cement, afraid of what others are saying about my bulging lump of a body.

The end of my story is a break from my obese past, which I chose not to continue, and the beginning of the present and future that I chose! Moreover, during this third part of my memoir, I will share some decadent and delicious personal recipes— some I've come up with and others that I've modified—which might help you to begin your new lifestyle.

We will have to go slowly, because otherwise the message is lost and your head might just explode. I didn't want our memoir (Yes! It is already yours, too!) to be just another diet book or another weight-loss book hanging out on the shelf. You know those books . . . the ones that tell us what to do until we discover that those regimens don't even work? Yeah, those! I wanted our memoir, and my laughable experiences, to be remarkable—but most of all, useful!

I will stop yapping now, which I will do a lot in this book, so that you can start.

To begin, we will have to travel close to nineteen years back into the past. So turn the page and let's begin.

Chapter 1

A Baby Buddha Was Born

September 12, 1991-1997

Boy, he'll be a great football player—so big and tall for his age.... Being overweight runs in our family; there's nothing to be done.... It's a problem with his metabolism.... Look at the chubby baby, those fat little legs—isn't he cute?

MY LIFE WAS A CIRCUS AND A COMEDY SHOW BY THE AGE OF three months: I was already the size of a one-year-old! I was hairy with big cheeks, big legs, feet akin to tamales and hands like over-stuffed, gone-wrong pita breads. Soon, everyone in the family started visiting me. I was the first boy, nephew, grandson, great-grandson of the family; and to top it all off, I was the first child within my parents' group of friends. Oh yeah! I was a total Super Star. In a way, I was like the Dalai Lama— everyone was coming to see me. And of course, they brought gifts! Being the first at everything—from the first at baby-farting and baby-burping to the first wearing Pampers—made the whole situation more of a spectacle.

One of the first few visits was from a friend of my parents— Elena (whom I later called Aunt Elena; we became that close!). My parents, Cecilia and Hugo, said that Aunt Elena came running into our house, ecstatic, jumping up and down, with a gift wrapped in baby Dalmatians-print. She also held a balloon that said "It's a Boy!"

As soon as Aunt Elena saw the big lump resting in the bassinet—in which I barely fit—she turned to my mom. Her eyes were about to burst out of her skull and her lower mandible almost touched the ground.

"What the hell did you eat during your pregnancy?" she asked. "This kid is huge!"

Then she began unwrapping the present. She showed my mom the newborn jumper. It was designed to fit a *normal* newborn. But only one of my sausage-like legs would have fit in that tiny outfit.

Aunt Elena wasn't done; just to dig herself into a deeper hole, she remarked, "I should've bought a jumper for a one-year-old!"

The size of a one-year-old, when I'd been around for barely ninety days? Did she mean me? Of course, it had to be me. At that moment, I became even more of an exhibition, if that were possible. Instead of congratulations or a hug, my parents got an unusable jumper, which was never worn, not even by my sausage-like leg. They also got to see a look of shock and hear "this kid is huge!" But my mom didn't mind. She responded by saying "Oh, but look at this cute baby!" as she kissed my feet.

This was the first but not the last time I got "This kid is huge!" I heard that same expression again when I was about nine months old, according to my mom. My Uncle Atto and Aunt Betty came to El Salvador to visit me. They were really excited to see me because, as I said before, I was the first nephew, and they wanted to spoil me rotten.

But surprise, surprise! They didn't expect this one, either. When they arrived at my house and saw me, my mom says, they gaped in shock. Then they asked that question again: "What the heck do you feed this kid? He looks almost a year and a half old! This kid is huge!"

My mom says that she giggled and said, "But isn't he cute? Look at those cheeks!" as she grabbed my cheeks as if they were stretchable balls attached to my face. My mom says that my uncle took his turn grabbing my cheeks and said "El gordito!"

El gordito is a Spanish expression meaning "little fat boy." Now, don't think that word was an insult; don't get it twisted! It was more like a cute nickname. Everybody thought it was a compliment! After that day, El Gordito became my identity. And believe me, sometimes, something inside of me tells me that nickname was especially created for me.

El Gordito became very popular. I became like a little fat golden child. I was like a baby Buddha. You've seen how in some families the attention is always directed toward a specific child, either because he was the first grandson or first nephew or first graduate or the first boy. In that family, that kid becomes "the golden child." Well, everybody was very interested in seeing me—and, of course, in playing with the rubber balls on my face. Their attention made me feel special.

At any reunion, when my mom entered the room, everyone would look up. They were not interested in her new outfit or her new highlights; they were interested in the thing she was carrying. They were interested in seeing my little "cute" tummy and my rosy, round cheeks. They would go right in for the kill, grabbing my tamale feet, my over-stuffed pita bread hands and my stretchable bouncy-ball cheeks, and then making farting noises by pressing their lips against my round, bare belly.

Was this behavior normal? Well, I guess it was somewhat normal for people to be interested in the spectacle coming in through the door. But after I was several months old, don't you think that attention would diminish? Don't you think the "cute" factor would fade away, just a tiny bit? Weirdly, in my family, my cuteness never left. Somehow, everybody was blinded by my plump tummy and my adorable, round cheeks.

As the years passed, El Gordito was still standing strong. Weirdly, El Gordito never went out of style. He was never replaced, much less forgotten. He went through twenty seasons and he was still present. But of course, eventually, everything must change.

The change that took place for me was not a change for the good.

By the time I was six, I was no longer a baby. The nickname El Gordito was a bit too cute by then. My family needed some spice, so my Uncle Atto decided to switch it up a bit. He decided to call me "Curly," after one of the characters in the Three Stooges. Curly was the funniest and the fattest of them all. He would wear his striped suit with his striped pants hiked up as high as possible—way up past his belly button. He would wedge his arms into the matching jacket, which was tight as well. I swear, when watching episodes of the Three Stooges, I was afraid one of Curly's jacket buttons would pop off, come through the television, and hit me in the eye—or maybe break a vase.

Thankfully, that never happened. Curly's jacket seemed stretchable and the buttons held on, as if by magic. Curly's magic buttons must have been strong, since they protected his belly from bursting out. Curly was hilarious. I laughed at everything he said and did. He was as awkward as someone could be, but his clumsiness was really funny.

I guess that growing up with a belly contained by a very tight Power Ranger shirt, combined with my natural awkwardness, made Curly the perfect nickname for a six-year-old boy—*right?*

In order to keep up with this new nickname, I had to upgrade! My hair was chopped off almost all the way to the root, just like Curly's. My shirts became tighter, as did my shorts. My belly became bigger—maybe that's why my shirts got tighter. My cheeks became fuller; my legs looked like turkey legs, as if they were ready to be eaten at Christmas dinner. My arms took on the proportions of Italian sausages. By that time, my new awkwardness began to shine. I was living *la vida Curly*.

I was living up to Curly's standards, and I was somehow able to pull it off.

I clearly remember one day when we were going to have a barbeque at my grandparents' house. I don't know why it was so important, but I knew I had to get a haircut and new attire. My mom went to the salon (which was rare), my dad shaved, and even my French Poodle, Negra, got fluffed up. I guess this barbeque was an important event.

Around ten a.m., my dad took me to the barbershop down the block. Obviously, we didn't want to get "tired," so we took the car—even though it was just around the corner.

When we got to the barbershop, it was empty. The owner told me to sit in one of the big, red chairs. The red chairs were used by adults. Like my dad. Big people. Old people. But I didn't want to sit on those chairs. I was only six and still a kid, so I wanted to sit on the kids' chair—which, by the way, had a life-sized Power Ranger cutout next to it.

I wanted to sit next to the red Power Ranger, who was my hero. I demanded it. I knew I was going to feel important sitting next to a super star like that—well, at least next to his replica. More importantly, I also would have an excuse to tell my friends that I had sat next to him. I might rub it in their faces a bit.

As the barber looked at me, his anxiety began to rise. I knew why he didn't want me to sit in the child's chair. That chair seemed a bit too small for a mini replica of Curly. My big butt and belly wouldn't fit in that chair, but he didn't want to point that out! I didn't feel insulted; I just wanted to be close to him, my favorite Power Ranger. I wanted to touch the Power Ranger or breathe his air or something!

Eventually, my dad ended the standoff. His façade turned to serious mode and he said, in his annoyed voice, "Just get in the red chair and stop bugging me! We don't have much time!"

So I gave a goodbye stare to my Power Ranger and walked away. My dad says that I got very emotional and made a "see-you-never" face. Finally, I slowly walked over to one of the big, for-old-people, red chairs and dropped my butt into it. The bald guy asked my dad how he wanted my hair to be cut. My dad simply answered, "The same," he didn't even bother to look up.

Twenty to twenty-five minutes later, I was done. I didn't even bother looking at the mirror. I just wanted to get out of there and go back home. My dad paid the barber and I was the first to get out the door, ignoring the barber's two thumbs up! At that moment, I didn't care about his fingers, though I wanted to give him one of mine.

As my dad tells it, I was so livid that I didn't even say the "magical word." Believe me, at that point, I'm sure I didn't care about manners. I wasn't about to say "thank you" to someone who had taken away my opportunity to sit next to my idol.

We got home and flew into preparations for the barbeque, dressing and packing and all that crazy stuff. Soon we were on the way to my grandparents, ready to party . . . and eat!

I rang the bell and they opened the door. Everybody had been expecting Curly, and that is what they got. I wore a short-sleeve, button-down, striped shirt with black, tailored pants and black shoes. Let's not forget the hair, now. My dad had told the barber to cut it "the same," so it was very short, almost shaved. Just like Curly's.

My Uncle Atto was the first to come out and greet us. He screamed, "Heeeere's Curly!" in a very circus-like voice. He sounded like I was about to give a show and he was my publicist. The only thing missing was the circus song and someone taking tickets at the entrance. Everybody turned around, and when they saw me, it was just as if they were singing a hymn. They chanted, in unison, "Awww . . . Curly . . . he's so cute!"

How come nobody noticed my tight shirt or my sweaty face or my jelly-like belly hanging over my tight pants? Nobody else seemed to care about those things. I mean, I knew I was bigger than other children, but it seemed as if something had blinded my family and made them believe that my belly was normal. My cousins, who were younger than I was, were called "handsome" or "pretty." Why was I, already six years old, still classified as cute?

Nobody seemed to acknowledge that my early "growth" might be a bad thing. They were so into hiding it by making it look cute or funny, they had forgotten it might be dangerous. It was like an Obesity spell. Obesity had blindfolded my family; he had made them believe that it was fine for me to be "plump," to say it in the nicest way.

Obesity said it was fine for me to have about ten extra pounds on me. It was fine for me to have a jelly-like belly that would jiggle every time I took a step. It was normal to be compared to an obese, forty-year-old comedian. My family was so blinded by Obesity that, instead of looking at the truth, they decided to make fun of it—and at some point, even hide it. Instead of being hard on me and trying to make me change my unhealthy diet, they decided to use me as a laughing matter, just like Curly.

I know it sounds a bit cruel, but Obesity had them eating from his hand. He also had me—unknowingly, but he had me. My family was an obstacle Obesity had to jump over to get to me, and clearly he had made a successful leap! It was like a true war! My family was a barrier that would have had to stop the enemy and protect me. Instead, Obesity had infiltrated into my family's army and manipulated them into believing that being overweight was healthy and cute.

Somehow, my family had not realized that my health was in danger—they had fallen deep into the misconception. Meanwhile, Obesity had them under his control. They didn't want to see that I was overweight, because they knew that I was still a young kid. If I already had an ailment as dangerous as Obesity, then the blame would have fallen on them. They were the parents and I was the child. I can see why they might have felt that way, but I would rather have seen them fight for me and try to stop Obesity, or at least not fall under his spell.

I was growing up. I didn't fit next to my Power Ranger at the barbershop. Of course, I wasn't just growing up; I was also growing out sideways.

Chapter 2

Manipulation
1998

IF THERE'S ONE THING I HATE, IT'S TO SEE KIDS CRY. THOSE SHRILL screams are just like the fingernails across a blackboard. Their squeakiness and high pitch make my ears bleed; believe me, I am not exaggerating.

I was part of that squeaky group. My cries were heard mostly in those infamous, wicked fast-food places. Those places target the little people until the children are living in the land of screams and tears, trying to get what they want.

I've been in junk food places millions of times. All junk food places are almost the same; the difference might be the choice of the tile floors or the different type of toilet paper in the bathrooms, but other than that, they're all the same. All these places have a 1,000-calorie meal, crappy baits, unenthusiastic people working at the counter and weird names for their combo meals.

None of this caught my attention until two years ago, when I began noticing what was taking place around me as I stood in line. The things that left me speechless were the screams made and the tears shed by kids, to the embarrassment of their parents.

Kids these days have been getting more demanding and pushy. Don't get upset if you were one of them—because I was one of them, too. Kids have become their parents' puppeteers. They decide where to go, what to do, what to get and when to get it. It's ridiculous to see how parents have stopped being the iron hand of the household; instead, children are taking control. But why has this happened?

I think I am a pretty good example that demonstrates why and how children begin controlling parents. With me, everything started with the "shit talk" from my doctor.

I was overweight by the age of seven, which was weird and unbearable in Salvadorian society. I remember my pediatrician, Dr. Something (I have never remembered his name) sitting with his clichéd white coat on his black leather chair, telling my mom every time we had an office visit: "This boy is too fat. Stop giving him shit to eat!"

Why did he get so mad, you may ask? First, I think he really cared about me. And second, I reflected his work. If I was fat, he wasn't being a good doctor! Does that make sense? The sad part is that he would give us the "shit talk," but he wouldn't *do anything* healthy about it. Of course, he would give me a new diet every time we visited him . . . but those diets didn't work. Dieting gave me immediate results, BUT it would stop working two weeks after I started. Sadly, I would gain the weight back. Then I would go back to eating my crappy food (which is what he used to call it).

It wasn't literally crap, the food my mom gave me, but it was what I wanted. My mom always tried to please, even if that meant letting me have 1,000-calorie meals. It was very hard to say "No" to a seven-year-old boy who started crying and screaming when he didn't get to eat what he wanted. I recall a trip to one of the most famous food chain restaurants when my "charm" won out over my parents' good sense—if what you'll read next can be called "charm."

I remember just pointing at the big yellow sign. My index finger had decided where to go and there was no way to make a u-turn and turn around. We couldn't turn to the left or right. What was said was said and what was done was done, without modification. My mom's input was ignored; the only decision that mattered was the one coming out of the kid sitting next to her.

We were driving toward the big, yellow "M" (you know what "M" I'm talking about; we've all been there). It was as if I were in the World of Oz, skipping down the Yellow Brick Road toward the headless master who was going to give a brain to my friend, The Man of Straw, and draw a smile on my hopeful façade by returning me to Kansas.

I always had a very bright smile when I was traveling on my Yellow Brick road, as well as an uncontrollable excitement. There was the jittering movement of my feet; it felt as if my feet were undergoing an epileptic seizure. Just to add to the tension, I'd ask the same question every five seconds: "When are we going to get there?" My excitement was so out of control that I almost jumped out of the car while my mom was still parking.

I was just thinking about the first bite—the bite that makes your mouth water. The bite that, in a matter of seconds takes you to another dimension.

We finally parked and I was able to unbuckle my seatbelt and run across the parking lot toward the door. I opened the door and the smell of french fries and apple pies went up my nostrils, waking up every sense that had been sleeping. My eyes nearly popped out, my knuckles began cracking and my feet moved in indescribable ways. My urgency to have my combo was almost unbearable.

As I entered the restaurant, I stared at the line and gave the people there a disgusted look. Three people stood between me and my meal. It seemed like a long line. I rushed to the front of the line, cutting in front of a woman and her son. I did it without saying "excuse me" or "I'm sorry." I just stepped in front of her.

She tapped me on my shoulder. At first, I wanted to go to the back of the line, which would have been the right thing to do. But at that moment, when I was so close to savoring my meal, I really didn't care what she thought. I kept a straight face and continued standing in front of her. I didn't even turn around.

Then my mom came in and asked me how I'd gotten so far ahead in the line. I was dying to answer "I'm quick," but the lady behind me jumped into our conversation and threw me under the bus by telling my mom what I had done. My mom grasped my wrist as tightly as she possibly could and dragged me to the back of the line. As she was pulling me along, I remember seeing the counter getting farther away from me. I was seeing my meal getting farther and farther away with each step. It was breaking my heart and, of course, my stomach. But I knew I couldn't do anything about it, so I resigned myself to being the last in line.

Instead of worrying about how far I was from my meal, I started looking at the menu, which was hanging above the lady who had betrayed me. Without a minute being wasted, I started telling my mom what I wanted. I pulled her down to my level and whispered,

- A cheeseburger (*Calories, 300; Calories from fat, 110; Grams of fat, 12*)
- A small soda (*Calories, 100; Sugar, 29 grams*)
- Large order of french fries (*Calories, 500; Calories from fat, 220; Grams of fat, 25*)
- For dessert, one chocolate fudge sundae (*Calories, 330; Calories from fat, 90; Grams of fat, 10; Sugar, 48 grams*)

TOTAL: 1,230 Calories; 510 grams of fat; 77 grams of sugars.

A 1,200-calorie meal for a seven-year-old?

Why did I want that? First and foremost, because it was the kid's combo meal, and that is what kids should get, right? And how could I say no to the big Power Ranger that came with the combo? Everything sounded so good and delicious.

The "shit" speech the doctor had given us twenty minutes earlier had entered my brain through the right ear and went out the left ear. Oh yeah, I forgot to mention that this visit to the fast-food place was right after a doctor's appointment. Go figure!

I was just blinded by Obesity, and I really didn't care. In my own seven-year-old world, it was worth eating all that. And let's not forget, my hands awaited the moment I could nurture that little red creature, my new toy. My palms anxiously itched and twitched in hopes of holding the Power Ranger—which was the attention-caller of the combo, the worm at the end of the fishing rod, the bait! Those little action figures couldn't have gone on with life unless someone fostered them. I was going to have a red Power Ranger, with his golden little belt and small white boots! Everything was the way it was supposed to be, the way it had to be.

My mom was on the way to agreeing. She looked at me and started nodding. She crossed her arms and kept nodding. Then she started reminding me about what the doctor had said. But at that moment, I didn't give a cat's stinky butt about that talk! I just wanted my combo. As my ears heard the word "no," my eyes began to water.

As she saw the first drops coming down my round cheeks, my mother, in a rigid and cold voice, said, "Do not make a show. You are not having all that. The doctor said you have to eat healthier! And you want all *that* food just because of the Power Ranger. Forget it!" My gaze dropped down to the floor and my heart began falling apart as my mom continued destroying my dream. I kept staring down as we stood in line—and I began plotting my comeback.

My mom was looking at the menu, but I was thinking about how to get my Power Ranger.

Finally, we arrived at the counter. My mom went first. She asked for what she wanted and then she looked up and told the lady, "I want something for him that's not that greasy . . ."

Not "that greasy"? We were in a fast-food restaurant . . . hello!!

I stared at the lady, who was listening attentively with her hand on the keyboard, waiting for my mom to order. In the split second that my mom stood there quietly staring at the menu, trying to figure out what to get me, I remember thinking, I want my french fries, and my sundae . . . and of course, my Power Ranger. It was my time to shine, like the weeping star that I was.

I started pulling my mom's pants. I pulled her pants so hard that she needed to hold them up.

"What do you want?" she asked, annoyed.

"I want my combo. I want my Power Ranger!" I screamed.

She kept nodding while I kept screaming and crying. We were holding up the line. People were staring at me, but I didn't care. I wanted to cry. Actually, I just wanted my fries, burger, sundae—and of course, the Power Ranger.

Was this going to be the first time I wouldn't get what I wanted? No! I dropped my butt to the floor and kept crying, pulling my mom's pants and kicking and pounding the floor. I was pounding my hands on those sad, gray tiles and my hands were getting redder and redder with each pound. My tears fell on the floor. I truly believed I was going to make a pond out of all my tears, in which I was going to, sadly, drown without my Power Ranger.

My screams were heard around the world—or at least around the restaurant. Just so you have an idea of how berserk I went, a kid who was maybe four or five years old came running over. He stared at me and asked his mom, "Is he okay?" The mom just yanked him away by the hand, saying, "Don't be nosy . . . he'll be fine."

By now, my mom was reaching her boiling point. Her face was as red as the Power Ranger I wanted. She always scratched her head when she was angry. She was now scratching it as if there were no tomorrow. I thought her scalp was going to fall off. She was fuming! I'm pretty sure her urine was boiling and her saliva was turning green. She was going crazy. Her eyes were like pinwheels.

And even though she was exploding, she was trying to keep her composure. It seemed as if she were about to cry. I just stared at her with a selfish look. I wanted what I wanted, when I wanted it; and that *when* was right there, at that moment.

Seconds later, the same kid who had run over to see my little "show" said, "Finally, it ended" as he let go of his ears.

My mom was giving in. She grabbed me by my arms, stood me up and whispered in my ear—in her angry no-nonsense voice—"What do you want?" Iron Hand had left the building! In the end, I got the 1,230-calorie meal!

My craziness, crying and begging—the show I put on for everyone to enjoy—was like a potion I could give to my parents whenever I wanted something. I'm pretty sure this happens in many families. It has become a phenomenon that makes parents fall under a spell. It begins with the first tear and it ends with the last scream. The scream that resonates in the parents' eardrums is the one that just makes them give up. Subsequent to the scream, a smile comes upon the kid's face, a smile that is victorious! The parents, upon seeing their kid so excited, become happy once again. They celebrate with him, but they seem confused, as if they don't know what just happened. This is the spell that makes parents go nuts for us. It's so easy for parents to fall under that hex.

After my mom whispered in my ear, asking for my order, I knew that I was getting what I wanted again. I told the unhappy lady behind the counter, "I want the kids' combo with the red Power Ranger and fries and the twenty-four-ounce coke and in the sundae—can I get chocolate fudge, too?" (That chocolate fudge part hadn't been in the original plan!)

My mom paid and we moved to the left. It had taken us about fifteen minutes to order, but it was worth it—or so I thought at the time. I got what I wanted! I got my fries, my cheeseburger, my sundae, my soda and my Power Ranger. But there was something I didn't get . . . What was it? Oh yeah, I didn't get any healthy food!

That was typical of going out to lunch with my mom. I got to eat whatever I wanted. Where I wanted. When I wanted. And it was all because my mom wanted me to be happy, due to her unconditional love. Yes! Unconditional love played games with my mom.

As I said before, the doctor's appointments weren't very helpful. Every visit was the same. The doctor blamed my mom for my bulging fat every time. I remember going into the little waiting room, which seemed older and gloomier with each visit. We would sit on an uncomfortable brown couch until the doctor came out and called us in.

His first words were always, "Stand there." In a matter of seconds, I was standing on the dreaded scale, looking at the black and white numbers rumbling around. Then he would ask me, "Your age?" and I would answer, "Seven" in a scared, fragile voice. He would write, "Only seven years old and 120 pounds."

When he'd gotten over his shock, he would start cornering my mom about my weight. In other words, he would question my mom's mothering skills. She would turn to me without saying anything and raise her eyebrow; trying to make me remember about the fast food I'd eaten after the last appointment. Thanks, mom, for not throwing me under the bus!

She'd smile, make jokes and try to diffuse the tension by changing the topic of conversation. They would start talking about the business, or the economy, or whatever adults talk about. My mom always avoided the really important conversation. She didn't want to tell the doctor that I had her all worked up. She didn't want to tell him about the shows I put on so I could get what I wanted to eat. She didn't want to tell him that she loved me so much that she wanted me to have what I wanted. She didn't want to tell him that she didn't know what to do with me.

My mother just wanted to get out of that room as fast as possible without dealing with the doctor's speeches. I do not blame her; I didn't like them either. But now that I think about them, I know we didn't like the doctor's speeches because we were afraid of the truth. We didn't want to see reality, much less accept it.

Ironically, at the end of the consultation he would offer me a lollipop.

Even if the doctor was trying to open my mom's eyes, it was impossible to make a change. I always continued with my bag of chips, my candy and my soda. That was my usual snack in between lunch and dinner. It was like a second lunch!

Every day, about two in the afternoon, my parents would drop me off at my grandparents' house. As soon as my seatbelt was unbuckled, I'd rush to kitchen and open the refrigerator and the counter drawers to look for something to eat. My nanny, standing by the kitchen door, would ask me, even though she already knew, "What do you want?" I didn't even have the delicacy to reply. Instead, I would simply smile as I grabbed cheesy puffs, M&Ms and a soda. This was a complete menu, constructed to perfection. It started with the cheesy puffs. They were powdery and a vibrant yellow/orange. Each one of them was so crunchy and salty. That was the appetizer. I would eat half of a large "Family Size" bag in one sitting.

I would open and empty half of the bag into a transparent bowl and admire each and every single puff. After my most devoted admiration, I contentedly grabbed the bowl and carried it down the flight of stairs, sat down on the first two steps and made myself comfortable. I was like a robot. I would grab two or three at a time. I would barely chew them when I was putting the next three into my mouth. It was like a race. My nanny would look at me, tell me to slow down and ask, "Why don't you save some for later?" I would stare at her with a why-are-you-in-my-business look. Then she would just walk away.

In less than ten minutes, the bowl was empty and clean. The cheesy puffs were all gone.

After I was done with the puffs, I would walk into the kitchen and open the big counter drawers to get at the candy. I always took out a bar of chocolate or a bag of M&Ms; I would walk back to the flight of stairs, I'd sit down and start chewing them like a horse eating hay.

Just like a bad magic trick, in approximately five minutes, the candy had vanished. As I had eaten the cheesy puffs, I also ate the M&Ms—like a robot. I would grab three or four at a time and I would barely chew them as I was already putting the next four into my mouth. Snacking became like a race against time.

After I was done with the chocolates, I welcomed the dessert: a twenty-four-ounce glass of Coke. I needed something to wash everything down.

I remember that once, while my nanny was filling the glass, I went to the bathroom to wash my hands and get ready for the holy soda. When I came back from the bathroom, I saw this tiny, eight-ounce glass filled with soda. I asked my nanny, "Whose is this?" and she answered, "Yours." I opened my eyes like an owl and I started crying, "I want the big glass, the one that has the Power Rangers on the front. I don't want this one."

She looked at me and said, "It's too much for you."

As I cried, I ran to the phone! I dialed 911-Mommy. "Mommy! This lady doesn't want to give me soda in the glass you bought me. Remember, it was five dollars, and I don't want you to waste those five dollars!"

My mom just giggled and told me to hand the phone over to my nanny. It took less than a minute before my nanny said, "Yes, it's fine, don't worry."

We went back to the kitchen and she filled the big Power Rangers glass. I smiled at her and she said, yet again, "It was for your own good, but here you go."

I didn't care if it was for my good or not; this was another win for me, so who cared? To finalize this second lunch, I would drink the glass of soda. Then I would start wondering what to do next. Of course, a spotlight came on over the television. You know what happened next: vegging out in front of the TV and getting bombarded with more fast-food commercials!

My grandma's house was a pretty big house with lots of space to play or run around. For a seven-year-old, it could have been heaven. There were no rules and enough toys for a lifetime! Occasionally, my cousins and I would play hide and seek. My cousins were like little rats. They would sneak into the smallest places they could find. They would hide in holes or in the laundry baskets or just behind the doors. They were so skinny they fit into amazingly small hideouts.

I was always the first one to be found. It was very hard to fit behind the doors without being noticed, or to squeeze under the bed, where I couldn't fit, or to crawl into the laundry basket, which I could have broken. It was very frustrating not being able to hide. So after the first round, I would just quit and sit in front of the television. Was this actually playing hide and seek? It took them like two minutes to find me, and it took me less than a minute to give up. Sometimes they would pretend that they didn't know where I was, when clearly they knew!

Believe me, even if I wasn't playing hide and seek, I could always be found sitting on a flight of stairs next to the kitchen.

When my mom would pick me up, she would ask, "Where is my Gordito?" Immediately, she would start walking toward the stairs. She knew where I was without even trying to look for me. As soon as she would catch a glimpse of my plumpness, she would ask with surprise—even though she knew all along—

"What are you doing there?" I would only smirk at her while I grabbed the dead bodies of my friends: Chips, candy and soda!

By this point, Obesity had not only blindfolded my entire family; it was already controlling them by using me as the manipulator. Yes! I would manipulate everyone around me, as if they were my servants, to get what Obesity wanted and needed to grow. I was the middle man. He knew he didn't have to work hard for his requirements, since he knew he could get them as soon as my parents heard my first scream or saw my first teardrop rolling down the stretchable balls on my face.

Obesity was my puppeteer; he just needed to move the strings. He was sitting back as his demands were being accomplished, and I was ready to simply cry and embarrass my parents for my entire life. He was living inside me. My eyes were bursting out in tears every time he needed something else. And my bulge was getting bigger and bigger. Wasn't he living the life? Smart, but sneaky and disgusting.

Nevertheless, that wasn't all. Crying and embarrassing them is nothing compared to what he did next. He took advantage of the unconditional love my parents have for me. He knew they would do anything to make me happy. He maliciously, intentionally, knowingly took advantage of their feelings. He used them and disposed of them like trash. Enough said!

Certainly, without any doubts at all, I would have loved for my parents to have broken through the blindness and not fallen under the spell that my childhood Obesity had over them. But I guess that's what comes with parenthood. They simply loved me for who I was and didn't care how I looked. They loved me just for being their child.

Chapter 3

I Might Look like a Balloon,
But I'm Not Inflatable!

September 12, 1999

"BIRTHDAY BASHES." JUST LETTING THOSE TWO WORDS ESCAPE my mouth gave me goose bumps. With my mother as a party planner, what else could a kid want? Our unbelievable parties became the talk of the town. Every year, we had a different theme, which meant dressing up the place to the fullest. One year it was theme from the *101 Dalmatians*; the next one was a *Power Rangers* theme; the next one was my favorite singing group, and so on.

Everything at my birthday parties was exactly the way I wanted it. Every single detail was there. Every theme meant new ideas, and new ideas meant intrigue. Intrigue meant more desire for September 12th to arrive. I don't know if it was desired by others, but in my case, the week before every birthday was a no-sleep-until-birthday time zone at my house. Just thinking about how my mom used to surprise me leaves me speechless.

Although every party was unforgettable, there's one that's glued to my mind. It was my eighth birthday party. It was the Tarzan-themed birthday year. Everything was about Tarzan. The invitations were about Tarzan, Jane and their elephant, Tantor. The piñata was a life-size Tarzan. The cake was Tarzan swinging through the vines, which were connected to the candles that were little trees; the cake looked like a 3-D Tarzanian jungle. The tablecloths and napkins were Tarzanian. My balloons said "Happy Tarzanian Birthday." How do I remember all of these details? The easy answer is, I have more than two hundred photos of this party. And my parents' memories!

The party was amazing! All of my school and neighborhood friends were there. My entire family attended. Even my dog came.

The Spanish Country Club was the ideal place to hold this party. The country club had two pools: one for the big kids with a ten-foot trampoline at the deepest end and one for the babies. It also had two sets of swings—on which I learned that head and floor do not blend—and a slithering, green, scaly slide, with twists and turns that traumatized me by planting the possibility that a snake could eat me. But most important, the club food bars that were open all day and night.

My party was at an outdoor room on the first floor with a frontal view of the swimming pool. There were about fifteen tables surrounding the piñata; each could hold about ten people. Each table was decorated with a Tarzanian centerpiece, along with a green tablecloth printed with vines. One table was dressed up only in white linen. That's where my presents were supposed to be seated.

Opposite the gift table, two food tables were set up. One held the main course and the other one had my cake. The first table seemed like an eruption of food. We had hamburgers and hot dogs, club sandwiches and a nacho station filled with chips, various dips such as guacamole, fresh salsa, sour cream, refried beans and mozzarella cheese. We even had a bowl of Pedigree dog food for my dog.

When it was time for lunch, we were all in the pool. My friends and I were having so much fun that, as we saw my mom approaching the pool to announce the meal, we submerged our heads underwater so we couldn't hear her. But of course, we didn't even last ten seconds under water. I remember all of us jumping out gasping for air, as if we were breathing for the last time, splashing water everywhere and holding on to the edge of the pool for dear life.

"Lunch is served!" my mom announced as we were trying to save our lives by gasping for air. We all rushed out of the pool and into the food line with our plates in hand. We were waiting and waiting . . . and waiting. My friends didn't mind waiting; they were too busy planning the game we were going to play after lunch. Honestly, I cannot tell you what game was next, because I had tuned them out. I was daydreaming about the hamburger I was about to eat. Paying attention to them seemed pointless. I just wanted my burger!

After waiting in line for more than ten minutes, I finally was right in front of the hamburger station. An illuminating, celestial light came over the hamburgers platter. My eyes wandered, looking for the juiciest, biggest burger of them all until I caught a glimpse of one of the burgers at the very top. It was brilliant; it was glowing! I got the juiciest and biggest one!

My dad, who was in front of me, had chosen a burger the size of mine. I'm like dad, I thought. Next, I moved two steps to the right and arrived at the golden platter of french fries. I grabbed a handful of them, snatched up a side of guacamole and ketchup, and exhaled a breath of relief. Then I moved out of the line and headed to the "Birthday Boy's Table," which was opposite the food and cake.

I ate my burger with so much passion that it inspired my mom to take a picture of me in which I'm staring at the burger with I-Love-You eyes. It looked like I was about to kiss the burger and ask it to marry me. I kept eating, and in a matter of minutes, I was done with both the burger and the fries. I had devoured them as if they were my last meal before the slaughter. My plate was clean. It was so clean it seemed as if nobody had used it.

I sighed and said, with great relief, "Ummm . . . that was good." And I smiled. My friends turned their heads and stared at me, asking me if I was already done. I proudly showed them my plate and, once again, smiled. I looked at their plates; each one still held half a burger or some nachos. I felt so proud. I sat there staring and smirking at them with a ha-ha-ha-I-finished-first look.

My friends continued talking about some water war, but I truly don't know what they said. Right after showing them my cleaned plate, I had tuned them out all over again! I had begun thinking and daydreaming about the burger I had just eaten. I was remembering the juicy patty in the middle of the buns, the melting cheese and the crunch of the onions and pickles. The tang of the mustard and the salty flavor of the fries. I was remembering every single bite I had taken. Every single bite had become everlasting. I was imagining myself eating it all over again. That day, I discovered that one hamburger was no longer filling.

Something was wrong, though!

Out of the blue, literally, I heard something or someone growl. The growling had interrupted my daydream. What a surprise when I discovered it was my stomach and that I was still hungry. My tummy, with every single minute passing, was rumbling and howling louder and louder. I had to do something.

So I did.

I stood up and wandered over to my parents' table and hugged them both as I told them, "Thank you! This party is super cool."

Every step toward the food table was like a milestone, as if I, instead of pressing "play," had pressed "slow-mo." I thought I was never going to get there. Finally, after what seemed like hours and hours of walking and eating my nails down to their nubs, I got to the food table. Thankfully, nobody had caught me in the act. I leered at the burgers. There were still a few left, so

I knew I would be able to get one without anybody noticing. I decided to go for it. I stretched my arm out and once again, out of the blue sky a hand fell, like a bag of bricks, on my shoulder, accompanied by a voice close to my ear. "What do you want?" the voice asked. I turned around to see my mom's face right in front of mine. Her puzzled eyes were looking right into mine. They were asking, "What are you doing?" Her eyebrows were close to her hair line, which meant she wanted an explanation. She knew what was going on. She was onto me, and this was not good.

"What are you doing?" she asked again. I put the burger down, very calmly, and I asked her if I could have another one.

She giggled. "Haven't you eaten, yet?" she asked. I nodded up and down.

She didn't bother to ask anything else. She just grabbed me by the hand and told me to go back and sit with my friends and "socialize." I stubbornly pulled my arm away from her and announced, "I'm hungry."

I went back to my table and began plotting my comeback. I had to do something to get my burger. I could cry and manipulate my mom. However, I was eight, and I couldn't kick and cry. My friends were present! They would have told everybody at school about my show. I would have been the talk of the town.

What was I going to do? Tick, Tock. Tick, Tock.

Wait a minute! Every outdoor room had a bar. In every bar, they sold burgers. I couldn't buy it at my outdoor room's bar, but there was a second outdoor room, and I was positive it had a bar. Plus, the bars were open the entire day, so I knew I had a chance to get my burger, and possibly even more french fries. But, there was another problem! How was I going to pay for the burger?

I thought for about a second on how to solve the problem; then I knew what I was going to do. First, I sat with my friends. I talked for a bit and grabbed my soda. I tried to socialize, to make my scheme less obvious. I drank the soda all in one sip and began pretending I needed to discharge, if you know what I mean. I turned to them and I started hugging my tummy. They asked what was wrong and I told them I needed to go to the bathroom. They laughed and said "Then go! Why are you here? We don't want your pee . . . or poop!"

I excused myself and started walking to the bathroom. At first, I was walking calmly—just like a duck, calm on the surface but paddling like crazy below. When I realized I was halfway there, I started fast-walking, like a crazy waddling duck. I fast-walked and fast-walked, pretending I was headed toward the bathroom.

When I reached the bathroom door, I looked back at my party, but everyone seemed to be distracted and having a good time. Instead of going into the bathroom, I went up the first step to the second floor and looked back. Nobody was looking. I went up one more step and looked back again—nothing!

I ran up the stairs as fast as I could, counting: three, four, five, six, seven, eight . . . fifteen. When I put both of my feet on the top landing, I looked back once again at my party. I was safe.

I walked to the counter of the open bar. The man behind it asked how he could help me.

"Can I have a burger?" I whispered.

He looked back at the kitchen of the bar and said, "You're a lucky kid on a lucky day! We just finished preparing one."

I smiled as he handed the merchandise over to me on a white plate.

"That'll be four-fifty," he said.

I didn't have cash, much less a credit card, but I knew my mom had an account at the club. "Can you put it under my mom's name? Her name is Cecilia Hidalgo."

Up and down his head nodded.

"So I'm good?" I asked in a hesitant voice.

"Yes . . . and by the way, I hope your mom knows what you're doing," he said.

I smiled and grabbed the burger. I didn't even bother to grab the plate. I wasn't planning on carrying the plate; it would have been too obvious. My plan was to shove the burger in my mouth and swallow it while going down the stairs, before arriving at my party. I was sure I was going to make it.

I started going down the stairs. This time, I wasn't counting. My burger was way more important than the number of stairs I had gone. I didn't notice when the stairs ended. I continued walking toward my party without remembering the burger in my mouth.

Suddenly, I heard someone screaming, "Curly!" and "Cheese!" At that moment, I knew there was going to be photographic evidence of my inability to fill my tummy with one adult-sized burger!

"What are you eating?" a squeaky voice asked. The voice was coming from behind my dad.

"I was hungry, I told you!!!" I screamed at the top of my lungs, half-chewed burger spewing out of my mouth.

"You ate a *whole* entire burger and now you go for the second one?" she asked. "Where did you get it? How and why?"

I simply stared back at the bar on the second floor.

My mom knew what I had done. Then she asked, "How did you pay for it?"

At first, I didn't want to tell her that I had decided to charge the burger to her. But something inside of me was telling me to confess. I had to. Her face was red, and she was standing close to me. I was scared. She was turning into a human tomato.

In a very low voice, I murmured, "I put it under your name."

"Great!" After a moment's pause, she said, "Just finish eating. Anyway, you're growing and you *are* a big boy. We're getting ready to cut the cake." She said this with an I-lost-the-battle voice. Then she turned her back to me and walked to the party.

I didn't get spanked—thank God! I did what I wanted. I got what I supposedly needed. I had such a huge alliance with food that it was extremely hard for me to break free. Obesity had made me dependent on food. I was eating so much now that Obesity had blindfolded and tricked my brain into believing that I needed to eat more and more to fill my tummy. Obesity was making my tummy stretch and stretch; and as it got bigger and bigger, it demanded more and more food. It had taken control over my stomach, my brain. It had complete control of me. It already controlled my mother, father and family members.

Chapter 4

I Go Cocoa Loco
1999

IT WOULD BE LOGICAL FOR YOU TO BE THINKING THAT, BY MY eighth year, my parents would have started noticing my jelly belly. It would be logical for you to wonder if my parents were plotting something against Obesity. It would have been *logical* for my parents and my family to start waking up from the Obesity spell they had fallen under.

I wished my family had done something about my eating disorder, but, sadly, they were still under the enchantment. Everybody around me was still under the spell, and there seemed to be no way of getting them out.

My parents were feebly trying to gain some power over Obesity, but they weren't successful. My dad was always trying to push me into sports. He dreamed of his son becoming a soccer star, just like he had been. One time, he bought me all the equipment to start my soccer career. I dressed up for a photo, but alas, once photo time was over, I went right to the benches and sat my Curly butt down. The only sports memory we have is of me posing for the camera, pretending I was a soccer player.

My mom had rebuffed some of my food choices. She didn't want me to eat more than I needed, but in the end, she gave up, just like she always did. She tried to sign me up for any type of physical activity available: karate, dance, swimming, basketball. It seemed as if my parents were trying to lead me onto the healthy path, but they were gradually giving up. Obesity took advantage every time they were at a vulnerable stage. Obesity attacked ruthlessly. But I guess he noticed that just attacking was not enough. He wanted to destroy me. A year before my eighth birthday, I had been crying outrageously for a Power Ranger that came with a 1,200-calorie meal.

Two years later, there I was in the cereal aisle, trying to decide which box to take home. There were several factors that affected my choice. First of all, I was short, maybe half as tall a the shelves. This meant I couldn't see what was on the very top shelf, so I could only choose from the middle on down. Furthermore, bright colors and chocolates were my attention-grabbers. I couldn't see far beyond them; bright colors make most kids happy.

I walked up and down the aisle three times, looking strictly at cereals at my eye level. Nothing caught my attention at first, but then . . . I saw something. There was a yellow and orange box with a picture of a red person and a bird.

As I approached, I recognized the image on the box, and it gave me goose bumps.

On the box was an orange bird with a yellow beak holding a bowl filled with small chocolate balls. He was smiling! He seemed happy. And next to the bowl, there he was! A picture of my idol: the Red Power Ranger. The picture showed him standing over a phrase that said, "Have a chance to win one!"

I wanted it!

I grabbed the box and really don't remember how long I stared at it. I just remember standing and holding it and admiring it, as if I were falling in love with it!

At last, my mom yelled "Are you done? Is that the cereal you want?"

I ran toward her and gingerly placed the box into the cart. She snatched up the cereal and asked me how much it cost.

"I don't know," I answered, "but I can win a Power Ranger! And at the top it says that it's good for me."

It did say "Energy source for kids" (or something like that) on the box, and I think that was the reason why my mom let me have it. She didn't even bother going to check on the price, which was rare. She just left it in the cart and headed to check-out number 5.

"Two-fifty! That's the price? Are you sure?" My mom seemed astounded as the lady working at the counter confirmed the price; but she seemed astounded in a good way. Two-fifty for a box of cereal? It couldn't get cheaper than that.

"Grab that bag," my mom told me.

She bought it!

The bag I grabbed contained the cereal box. I smiled and headed to the car.

The next morning, the first thing I did was open the box and serve myself a big bowl of that cereal. I really didn't want to eat it, but I wanted to finish it to see if I had won my idol. I didn't!

"That's okay," my mom said. "Next week maybe you'll get it."

Next week? I thought to myself: This means she's going to buy it again! Let me tell you something: despite the fact that, at first, I had only been interested in the Power Ranger, the sugar high that I got from that cereal was unbelievable! The sugary feeling would go down my throat every time I would eat it and magically start relaxing and relieving me. I was able to inhale and exhale in a serene manner. And I liked it! It was a party in my mouth!

The following week came, and she bought that cereal again, and then again the week after that, and the week after that, and so on. Every week was the same motion picture. We would enter the big red door and she would let go of my hand. I would run directly to the cereal aisle and grab the Cocoa Loco box that was waiting just for me! The only difference from one week to the next was the prize. One week it was the Power Rangers, the next week it was Star Wars, the next week it was Pokémon, and then the Flintstones, and then the Supersonics, and so on. The prizes changed, but since all of those television shows were popular then, all of them called my attention—and not only my attention, but my friends' attention, too. We could have made a Cocoa Loco club!

I became addicted to that cereal. I was cuckoo for Cocoa Loco. Every morning, I didn't even have to say what I wanted. Everybody knew that I needed to have my Cocoa Loco fix; otherwise, it would be war. I wasn't only choosing which fast-food place to go to; now I was choosing what I was going to eat at home, too.

After a while, Obesity had to start working outside restaurants. He had to expand. He needed to penetrate and leave his legacy on a place where families buy most of their food: the supermarket. That is how he entered (drum roll please) the supermarket industry!

Little did my parents and I know that supermarkets place the products targeting children on the lower shelves, at their eye level. There's where all the brightly colored cereal boxes, the ones based on children's television shows, are displayed. And they are the ones with the highest fat, sugar and salt content! And these, too, are the cheapest ones. The healthy cereals are up on the top shelves.

When supermarkets work with Obesity, they sell more unhealthy foods, and more families take Obesity home in their shopping bags. That means Obesity gets closer and closer to more families, communities and countries. He continues growing, just like what he is: a malicious and injurious ogre who feeds from everyone to stay alive.

Chapter 5

I Go to Diet Concentration Camp
2000

"LOOK AT YOUR BOY; SO WELL-FED AND ROBUST! YOU SHOULD BE a proud momma."

"What do you give him to eat? Just look at him, so well grown!"

People all said the same things to my mom.

Adults really thought I looked healthy. Every time we would meet my parents' friends, they would congratulate my mom for having such a "robust" and "well-fed" child. The meaning of robust is: healthy, hearty, energetic and strong. But I wasn't any of those. Actually, I wasn't healthy at all. Hearty . . . I don't think so. Energetic . . . nope. I always chose the most sedentary activity. Strong . . . not! Even though I looked big, that didn't mean I was strong. My legs were so weak that I wasn't able to last an entire period at a school basketball game. I always had to be pulled halfway through.

Whatever these friends said, my pediatrician was saying otherwise. He always worried about my family's history of heart disease.

Although my pediatrician was concerned, he wasn't traveling on the right path, either. His intentions were noble, but his ideas—or should I say, his procedures—were not. He might have tried to persuade my parents multiple times, but I wasn't feeling it; so I was not buying it.

The doctor became like my parents' Bible. He was their law, their regime, their Communism. If he said "jump," they would jump. If he said "sleep," they would sleep. If he said "put Alberto on a diet," they would try to do so.

But he, like most doctors, was not well-educated about a new and growing disease: Obesity.

Obesity, in El Salvador, was unheard of. Therefore, trying to stop the problem was a special challenge. They didn't know Obesity's moves and methods, much less what he was made of. They didn't know how he disguised himself; they didn't know he even existed. His birth and evolution were all new to them. Because of this, all the methods that my doctor used failed.

By the age of nine, I had gone off the rails. I had already put on about ten to fifteen extra pounds. Additionally, by the age of nine, I had been on more than nine different merciless and waste-of-time diets! My parents tried them all on me, from the water to the tuna to the fruit to the vegetables diet. Been there, done that. On every doctor visit, a new diet would be thrown in my face like a cold bucket of water. Everything started with my pediatrician's sardonic speech about my growing fat. Following the useless speech, he would toss a thin, white piece of paper on my mom's lap. The paper listed all the things I was going to eat at every meal, for at least two weeks!

I had become a laboratory rat! The doctor was testing me with every diet available. He wanted to see if I could tolerate them. I had become something to play with. And let's not forget, these diets were physically tiring and, taste-wise, disgusting. They also tired me emotionally; I ended up crying every day because I didn't want to eat what "the list" said.

On top of it all, the diets were a waste of money. My parents would have to run to the nearest supermarket right after each consultation and buy two whole weeks' worth of "special" food for the "special" kid. Overall, each diet would take a toll on my parents and me.

But the hardest part for me was the lack of support from my family. Every diet was like being put in a food concentration camp. Everyone else, including my pets, would enjoy normal, human food: chicken, meat, beans and rice. I was the only one on the diet.

Of the countless diets, there was one in particular that really screwed me up . . . and the faucet and the toilet, too! This is how the first two weeks unraveled.

It started with a piece of toast, spread with a minimal amount of jelly. Then, a glass of water, a glass of milk and a glass of juice. All that liquid at 6 a.m.?

Obviously, my pediatrician was simply trying to fill my stomach with liquids. How healthy could that be?

But let me give you a bit more insight into a normal day on the Liquid Diet. I would come down the stairs, right about six in the morning, and see a vacant, white plate. In front of the plate, I would see three glasses. I'd sit down. That breakfast would be the dullest one I had ever eaten. I would eat my piece of bread, and my stomach would still be growling. How to stop that? With the milk, juice and water. I'd chuck those three glasses down my throat. I pretended to fill up.

Immediately, my stomach would growl even louder—and without delay, the bathroom awaited. I would open the door, and when I sat down, everything came out. The milk, the juice and the water would fight in my stomach. This War of the Liquids gave me a big case of diarrhea, every single morning, for two weeks. It felt as if I was vomiting from my behind. It was like a faucet was open and everything was coming out. Believe it or not, my butt crack got a rash from so much "cleansing."

After the flood, I would get ready for school, thinking that it was over. What I'm going to tell you next occurred every single day, too! As I was getting into the car, another growl would come alive. I wouldn't say anything. I knew what that meant, but I'd think I could hold it until I got to school and could use the bathroom there. I'd feel a cold rush through my body. Goosebumps would take over. My stomach would be hurting and growling and my arms would be hugging it, chokingly, trying to calm the ache. It wasn't going away and I couldn't hide it any longer. I had to tell my mom.

"Go!" she'd say as I was running out of the car, racing toward the stairs. I would sit again, and this time it would be worse than the first time. It was a nonstop shower. I felt like my guts were coming out.

For two weeks straight, I would get to school at least five minutes late. The first day, embarrassingly, my mom had to walk me down to my classroom and explain to my teacher what had happened. I didn't want a detention or to have my teacher take a point out of my attendance record. But at that moment, I really didn't care what she thought; I was just so worried about having another of those urges.

After everything came out of my body, I went hungry for two hours until snack time at school. I sat through history and mathematics thinking about food and hearing my stomach growl. I'd embrace it with my arms and trying to calm my hunger, as if it were an enraged lion try to get to its prey. Just picture me, with a chair and a whip, dressed up as Curly, trying to calm him down. And trying to pay attention to the teacher was another challenge. I was starving!

The first couple of days, when my friends heard my stomach growling, one of them turned around and laughed while the other one offered me a chocolate to calm my hunger down, but I had to refuse. I couldn't eat a chocolate. It would have broken my diet!

Time went slowly, but finally, my first recess would come. I used to call it "Snack Time." It was very simple and boring. For a snack, I would have some pieces of carrots with cottage cheese, unsalted, with no flavor or color. Just some pieces of carrots for a snack? Sure, they contain vitamins, but I am pretty sure five carrot pieces are not equivalent to even one serving. Those ruthless portions, dictating the beginning of my new starved way of living!

After my "snack time," my hunger would multiply by three. First, I was already hungry from breakfast. I had nothing in my stomach, and I was supposed to fill it up with a few pieces of carrots and a spoonful of cottage cheese? Then I had to wait two more hours to get out of school and go home so I could eat lunch? I thought I couldn't make it.

On top of all that, I had to deal with my annoying friends making fun of me because I was on a diet. They would bring out their sandwiches and milk or orange juice while I was sitting next to them with my tiny little carrots. They rubbed their snacks in my face, and I just had to suck it up and deal with it. I would try to laugh about my life, too. I'd pretend I didn't care. Acting as if my life was a comedy was the best defense mechanism I could find. I would tell them that only cool or famous people were on diets. Who the hell was I, back then? Nobody knew me. But I had to take the attention away from my dull life.

Sometimes, I had to just hide my carrots and then throw them away, so my friends wouldn't laugh at me. But by doing that, my hunger level went up two hundred percent! That meant I'd have headaches during English class and bad breath by science. By the time lunch came, I wasn't even hungry. . . I was mad, grumpy and resentful of my doctor. I was hating every minute of my life, and my stomach was growling every second. I didn't know if I was going to be able to handle this for two weeks. It felt like a sacrifice I was making every day.

Finally, lunch would come: a big, white plate plus a six-ounce chicken breast and a spoonful of vegetables equaled my lunch. That was it! No dressing! No rice! No bread! No dessert! No juice, only water! I had zero rights about what I got to eat. My starvation level would go down to about fifty percent after lunch, but I knew that waiting five hours until dinner—with no snacks in between—was going to be torture. No fruit. Nothing between lunch and dinner.

I had to psychologically prepare myself for it. I had to talk myself through it and calm myself down. But my resentfulness grew greater and greater by the minute. I hated everyone. I hated myself for being "the problem." I hated my parents for not understanding me and for falling into my pediatrician's traps. I hated my doctor for putting me through diet after diet. I even hated my friends because they were healthier and thinner than me and I couldn't be like them. I hated life.

Finally, five hours later, dinner would come around. But that just made me hate myself even more. Can you imagine how bad it was? Dinner was just like lunch; the only difference was that I had to wait the whole night to eat my bread and drink my three glasses of water, juice and milk. And believe me, I was not looking forward to another crazy-pooping time like the morning!

These events took place for two weeks. But of course, two weeks weren't enough. My pediatrician decided to keep me on the diet for another two weeks. I was hating my life to the fullest! You may be thinking that I was skinny as a toothpick after a month on this regimen. You are wrong! A month went by and I barely dropped five pounds. Only five pounds!

After that long month, my parents decided to take me off of the diet. It was not working, I was always hungry, and I didn't seem healthy. So my pediatrician seduced them into putting me through yet another diet. And they fell again for his smooth talk, and they accepted the next white piece of paper. At that time, I never thought that eating so little was unhealthy. My parents had taken it as the norm.

Everybody says that diets are the best way to lose weight, but diets are the worst experiments human beings have created and implemented in their lives. Read the following words carefully and engrave them on your brain: DIETS DO NOT

WORK! Diets suck. Diets are unhealthy. If you want live a star-vation-a-la-mode life, use a diet! Be my guest. But I got bad news, the "miraculous" results you wait for will never come! You will waste your time and energy!

Once I got off the diet, I regained the five pounds, plus an extra two, just to make my life more miserable and to make me feel worthless.

Chapter 6

I Am Swallowed by a Hammock
September 2002

MY DAD HAD MOVED TO CALIFORNIA WHEN I HAD JUST TURNED ten. He had been living in California for a year already and said it was "amazing, unimaginable and *cold* during the winter." Now it was our turn: my mom and I were going to join him in California, exactly two months after my eleventh birthday.

My grandparents decided to give my mom and me a good-bye feast at their beach house. Everything was set and ready to go. We would have two days of celebration. Uncles, aunts, grandparents, cousins, the dog and the beach—what else could I have asked for?

At around six in the morning our excitement levels were off the charts. We packed food, games, a cake, candy, chips, soda, balloons and a lot of energy and love into our car.

At around seven-thirty, we jumped into the car. My mother said it was just "a matter of minutes" to get to the beach house. It took us one hour and a half to get to our destination. We drove and drove. In my mind, I was going crazy, thinking we would never arrive! The traffic was horrible. Horns were being honked, vendors were crossing the streets and dogs were walking everywhere. This was a normal day in the traffic world of El Salvador.

On top of my extreme anxiety, add the delicious smell of food in the car. I was going crazy. I just wanted to jump on the food and eat it! But that wasn't all. Now add a cake to the mix.

Not just any cake. Imagine Curly and *the* cake. Yes! Cake, anxiety, and me, stuck in a car. It was not a good scene. Ironically, I was the person carrying the cake. I had the chocolate fudge cake on my lap. It was covered with vanilla frosting and decorated with fresh strawberries. In a word, it was torture. I just wanted to plunge into the cake and devour it, as if there was no tomorrow!

Finally, at around 9 a.m., I caught a glimpse of my grandparents' beach house. We had arrived.

The garage door opened and I entered a magical world. Green everywhere. Trees. Flowers. Ready-to-eat mangoes. Banana trees overflowing. Coconut palm trees bending over, since each had over ten ready-to-eat coconuts on it. The fresh air. The crystalline pool water. On top of it all, the cake I had on my lap. Everything was ready. It was just a matter of putting the balloons up, taking out the food and jumping in the pool.

An hour after we arrived, Uncle Atto and his family and Aunt Lorena and her family got there. My cousins ran out of their cars toward the pool, taking their shoes and shirts off and jumping like grasshoppers. I was waiting there, with my blue swim trunks and my white T-shirt. Yes . . . my white T-shirt. I couldn't go in the water without it. I would feel naked.

As soon as our feet touched the water, the fun began. But, in a matter of minutes, they called that lunch was ready. I couldn't believe it. The feast was about to happen. We ran toward the table, which was overflowing with food. It was loaded with burgers, sandwiches, fried chicken, pizza, *pupusas* (Salvadoran specialties), rice and beans, sour cream, sodas, chips and french fries. Let me put it this way: the table was for twelve people, but it held enough food for twenty.

I grabbed a burger, opened it up and poured mayo onto one bun and mustard onto the other. Of course, I added a side of fries. They were a golden brown and brighter than the sun.

Finally, I turned to the soda station, filled up and headed to the hammocks.

At the beach house, there was a corridor made especially for hammocks; it was like a hammock parking lot. That is where we settled after loading our plates. But getting into a hammock with a full plate of food and a drink requires special coordination. My favorite hammock was covered with yellow, red, green and orange stripes. I got to my hammock and sat down. But something was different this time. Somehow, when I sat down, my hammock seemed lower than usual. "Oh well, maybe it's not hooked up well," I said to myself. I looked up to where the hammock was hooked, but everything seemed to be in place. I let it pass and forgot about it.

I dug into my plate, as if I were being prepared for the slaughter, like a turkey fattening up for Thanksgiving. My cousins were eating like normal people. As usual, I was done first. I stood up and went back to the table. I wandered around for few minutes, deciding on what to eat next.

I locked my eyes on the table and saw one of my best friends sitting there alone, with no one to talk to. I stretched out my arm and I grabbed the burger. I placed it on my plate, but, in my eyes, it continued to look lonely. Just a burger on a white plate? That didn't seem right. I had to accompany it with another handful of crispy french fries. I poured some ketchup on my plate, next to the fries, and refilled my soda cup. Now everything was the way it was supposed to be.

I heard voices approaching. I moved to the pillar, poked my head out again, and caught a glimpse of Uncle Atto. He was saying "Curly!" Other family members were approaching as well. Their voices were getting closer and closer, and my butt was about to get caught.

I knew I shouldn't be getting more food, so I grabbed my plate and my soda and fast-walked toward my hammock. I had to act like nothing was happening. I knew I had to sit and just pretend that I wasn't there, fade in the background. When I was a few steps from the hammock, I heard loud voices at the table. They had reached the table; that meant they were closer than I had expected.

As I was sitting down in the hammock, I heard a tearing sound. While I was shocked from the sound, Eduardo asked me, "You're going to eat more?" I nodded, up and down, and shushed him. But yet again, I heard the tearing sound; this time it sounded closer and louder, and it was coming from my butt. I must have farted, I thought. My family was approaching the hammock corridor, heading to their siestas, right where I was getting ready to eat my second burger. In a matter of seconds, the soda fell on me. The cold liquid invaded my trunks and then made a pond on the ground. I felt like I had just peed on myself. Then the burger opened up and fell on my chest. I had yellow and white circles on my shirt. The patty was lying on the ground and the fries were flying off the plate; my dog was trying to catch them.

My cousins started laughing, and I felt a big rush of blood to my face; I bet my cheeks were as red as the ketchup. The hammock had ripped. As I was sitting down, the hammock had started ripping from the middle, exactly where my butt was. A hole had opened up and it was swallowing me. My butt was hanging out through the rip, and I was struggling against gravity. I didn't want to fall and was trying to save my food—even though, by then, it was all gone.

There was nothing I could do. I couldn't pull myself out of the hole . . . with what strength? Every sudden movement seemed to make the hole bigger. *Help!* My cousins were laughing so hysterically, they ignored my worried face and my calls for help.

The time had come. I couldn't do more, so I just let myself go. I was about a foot-and-a-half above the ground. I knew it was going to hurt. Finally giving in to gravity, I let myself fall through the hole. My butt hit ground first, followed by my hands. Then my back landed in the puddle of soda. The back of my head smacked against the tile. Above me, the remains of the hammock hung in two pieces. My dog had jumped on top of me and was licking off the mustard and mayonnaise.

"What happened?" my mom screamed.

Uncle Atto turned and said, "Curly fell!"

Everyone was laughing—even my dog. I couldn't blame them. The scenario was too funny. I would have laughed. A meatball-shaped kid on the floor with all that food on him, with the dog eating off him and the hammock split in two? Who wouldn't have laughed?

At last, my dilemma touched my cousins' hearts and they got up and tried to help me. I was too heavy for them. My dog jumped off me and ran away to eat the hamburger patty somewhere else. My uncle and mom approached and helped me get to my feet. My uncle pretended to study the hammock, but realistically, what could he have been studying? There was nothing to study. The hammock had ripped in two because I was too heavy, and I was on the ground covered with my second plate of food.

My uncle got on a chair and unhooked the two hooks at the ends of the hammock. I was cursing that hammock like there was no tomorrow. I was crying. My head was hurting. The sound of my head pounding the ground was still resonating in my ears. My back was burning red from the fall. My mom was hugging me, but I could feel that she was still shaking with laughter. My cousins were laughing. My uncle was still announcing that Curly had fallen. Everybody seemed very calm about it, but I was trying to cry louder to call attention to my pain. Somehow, everybody had tuned me out.

"It was old," my uncle said. "I think that the material was rotting. Anyone could have ripped it, but I guess Curly was the lucky one."

The hammock wasn't old. I knew that for a fact. I had bought it with my grandmother a year prior to my fatal landing.

My family kept reminding me of my perfect landing that entire night and the next day. They kept making fun of it and my cousins kept recreating the scene. They were not letting it go. What could I do? Just laugh! The party continued . . . as well as the overdone anecdote.

I would be leaving in a matter of weeks. Obesity had taken a toll on all of us. He was making me grow bigger and bigger, sideways. My thoughts had been manipulated and my family had become naïve about my situation. I was physically and mentally deformed, but Obesity had managed to cover that up. He had manipulated every single scenario that could have opened my family's eyes, like the hammock incident, for instance. Suspicion wasn't in my family's vocabulary, much less the word Obesity. They had hidden my weight problem by calling me "cute" names like Gordito and comparing me to famous stars, like Curly. Somehow the cute names plus the comparison with famous people made my size okay.

Obesity had put rose-colored glasses on us, and we couldn't take them off, since we didn't even notice them. We were living the life that he had chosen for us: a life in which we were crumbling little by little while he was enjoying it.

Chapter 7

A New World
November 2002

"4F?" I ASKED. IMMEDIATELY, THE ATTENDANT'S INDEX FINGER pointed at the seat in front of me as her eyes rolled back in a gosh-how-dumb-can-you-be expression. I felt embarrassed and didn't even say "thanks." Instead, I pulled my mom's hand and dropped my butt, like a bag of cement, onto the blue seat.

The moment I sat down, my mouth began running. "How long is it going to take from here to there? When are we going to get there? Who's going to be there?" My mom, who was frustrated after the sixth time I had asked her how long the flight was going to last, told me "Gordito, it's going to take six hours."

I started to fidget a bit, trying to make my butt comfortable. Then I asked for the seventh time. I was ready to arrive, but the plane's engines hadn't even turned on! We sat there awaiting departure for forty-five minutes. Finally, the loudspeaker turned on and a voice said, "Welcome to Flight 561, destination San Francisco." I squeezed my mom's legs as her arms went around me. A tear rolled down her face and landed on my head. She was happy about the start of our new life. She knew a better life full of opportunities, happiness, harmony, security and love, was forthcoming—but she was also giving up her family. It was a bittersweet moment.

Deep inside her heart, she knew this move was going to change our lives. And it did! Right before the front end of the plane began to lift off from the ground, she inhaled deeply and sighed. Six hours later, the voice announced through the very-loud speakers, "Passengers, please fasten your seatbelts. We will be landing at San Francisco International Airport."

I was looking out the window and admiring the San Mateo Bridge, so large and illuminated. The bridge was a radiant jewel, and next to it was the pearl of the night. People say that the moon looks like a pearl hanging from the sky. I could have almost touched it, but I was too busy eating the last piece of my mom's cookie.

We had been sitting for six hours. I had watched two movies, and it was 11:30 p.m. I was enormously excited to enter a new world, to step on new land. I thought I was ready to start a new life, even though I didn't know what was in store for me.

At the airport, everyone around me was speaking a language I didn't understand. Plus, I didn't know anything about the country. I hadn't yet learned that the United States was made up of fifty states and that it had traditions such as Thanksgiving and Labor Day. I didn't know anything about anything in my new world. My mind started foreseeing my first time going to a supermarket, my first day walking down the street, my first day going to McDonalds and my first day at my new school! Everyone was going be speaking English—how was I going to communicate?

As we were coming out of baggage claim, I saw two hands waving at us. I ran toward my dad and hugged him. He was giving me a welcome-to-your-new-home hug, but I was giving him a please-protect-me hug. I was still shaken up, and I just wanted to be with people I knew.

By the time we arrived in San Francisco, my dad's entire family had been living there for two years. They all were welcoming and nurturing as they waited for us, standing next to my dad with their arms open. It did feel good seeing all of them and identifying them as my new family.

Finally, after our eight bags had been haphazardly stowed in a green truck, we climbed in and drove off. About thirty minutes later, right when my head was bobbing around and my eyes were about to shut down, I was standing in front of a green door: the door to my new home. The wet-paint smell seemed very recent. The odor came to represent my new start.

The apartment was a bit empty, though: it had only a sofa, a television and a lamp in the living room. The single bedroom held two beds with a night stand in between, delineating my parents' territory and mine. From the get-go, I knew this space was smaller than what I was used to, but somehow, I immediately learned to like it.

It was cozy! It felt like a nest, a protective nest.

"Why are we going to eat turkey? Is it Christmas already?" I asked my mom. The day after we arrived was Thanksgiving.

She sat down and tried to explain the origins of Thanksgiving: something about some pioneers and the country and turkey.

I didn't get it and I didn't care. I was fixated on only one thing she had said: I was going to be eating, in couple of hours, a hot piece of turkey and a slice of apple pie with whipped cream on top.

Right about five in the afternoon, we arrived at my dad's family's house. Everyone was waiting for us. Some seemed happy to see us, and others seemed uninterested. Personally, I kind of felt out of place, like an invader. But as soon as I walked through the house and the fragrance of roasted turkey started invading my nostrils, I began to relax. As soon as I caught a glimpse of the fully loaded table, everything seemed tolerable. The twenty-five-person roasted turkey sat squat in the middle, with a brown gravy bowl next to it. And at the end of the table was a pie! I knew it was going to be a good night!

Weeks passed. The day I had dreaded since the moment the plane landed was rapidly approaching: going to an American school. It was time to prepare myself. My mom took me to buy some new clothes. She also bought me a new red backpack, four skate-boarding binders—I wasn't even fond of skateboarding, but I thought they were going to make me look cool—plus new Michael Jordan tennis shoes.

Everything was ready, but my anxiety levels were over the top. Finally, the dreaded day came.

"Hurry, you're going to be late!" My mom called to me from the car, where she sat watching me approach the big, brown door. I was extremely nervous as every worrying thought came to mind in a matter of minutes.

I was wearing blue jeans, my new Jordan tennis shoes, a gray, long-sleeved shirt and my yellow cock-a-doodle-do rain-coat. Nature wasn't operating in my favor that day. It wasn't raining cats and dogs; instead, it was raining dead birds, pine cones and a few branches. And the cold was not only smacking against my turkey legs and my hands, it was freezing the stretch-able rubber balls on my face. The cold was intolerable. I turned around to wave "goodbye" to my mom as she was driving away. It was a very pitiful picture.

I grabbed the brass handle and opened the brown door. In a matter of seconds, not only my cheeks were frozen, my entire body was as well. People were walking all over the place: going right, left, up and down. Some were ignoring the bell and wel-coming each other to a new semester. Others were running to their classes. Others, weirdly, were holding their pants up with one hand, not letting them fall.

Girls were putting on lipstick and painting their eyebrows with a black Sharpie. Others were running out the door, skip-ping the first day of school. And, I was standing there wearing my yellow coat and my white and red Jordan shoes, frozen in time, mind shut down.

A second bell rang. I knew my first class was about to start. I didn't have to ask what the bell meant; I pretty much understood it as soon as I saw everyone running toward their class-rooms.

I opened my schedule, which said: "First period: English-ESL." What is ESL? I wondered.

"Excuse me, where's this room?" I asked a guy who was hold-ing his pants up. I asked it in Spanish as I showed him my schedule and pointed at the room number. The expression on his face became putrid and he seemed to almost explode when he replied. I knew he was saying something, but I don't remem-ber what he said, since at the time, English was unknown to me.

Of course, my face blanked—but I could tell by his face that he wasn't thrilled to see me. His expression said it all. I kept walking until I saw the first signs of my classroom. How did I get there? Don't ask!

Almost a minute before class started, my feet touched English-ESL's ground. I entered the room and began examining the situation. The room wasn't that bad. It was completely white with colorful posters of the most famous writers on the wall, from Camus to Sartre to Gabriel García Márquez.

The teacher's desk, which was as brown as coffee, sat in front of the class, facing the students. Five rows of desks for students—with blue chairs to accompany them—stretched out in front of her. The setup was pretty simple. I guessed it was the American way.

Obviously, I wasn't going to choose a seat in the first row! Are you crazy? I walked directly to the last row and sat on the aisle seat, just in case I had to run away. I didn't want to be noticed. I just wanted to be invisible. The bell rang, and my teacher, Ms. Morgan, stood up and said, in both English and Spanish, "We have a new student!"

At that moment, I wanted to crawl under a rock and hide! Some of my schoolmates had turned around to look at me, sizing me up from head to toe. Some had said "Hi," and others didn't even bother looking. As I was absorbing all their reactions, my new teacher gave me the first request: "Stand up and present yourself."

I got so frightened, I froze up again. My legs began shaking, I cracked my knuckles and I'm pretty sure I felt something wet in the seat of my pants.

"Albert?" Ms. Morgan said as I was waking up from my second freeze. My name was the least I wanted to say. What was running through my mind was the following: "First of all, my name is Alberto; and second of all, I think I just crapped my pants!" Obviously, I couldn't say that; I didn't want to be the creepy kid. Instead, I pushed my butt off the chair, got to my feet and folded my hands on the front of my buckle. I began introducing myself, in Spanish. Within the blink of an eye, Ms. Morgan stood up and stopped me. Had I done something wrong?

She said, "Try in English,"

My cheeks were about to burst and my legs kept shaking. I took my jacket off, cleared my throat and thought, Here we go, English. Be nice!

"M-y n-a-m-e i-s A-l-b-e-r-t-o," I said slowly. Embarrassing!

The teacher applauded and said, "Job well done! You may sit down."

What had she said? What was I supposed to do? I didn't know. She had forgotten my disability. Thus, I stood, with my hands interlocked in front of my buckle, and my armpits sweating, for an extra ten seconds. Finally, with a wave of her right hand, she indicated that I should sit. Great! Another embarrassing moment. Curly was on a roll.

As I was sitting, I heard some of the students giggle and others whisper. I looked down at my paper and pretended I was working on something; which was an idiotic move, since only the first few minutes of my first day of school had gone by. Everyone else knew there wasn't anything to work on yet!

I sat there for the rest of the class, pretending. I wanted the day to be over. I just wanted to run to my apartment, lie down under the covers and hide. I just wanted to be in a place where I wasn't a stranger. Believe me, the thoughts of jumping out of the window and running away, or pretending to go to the bathroom and escaping school from there, crossed my mind. But there was one problem: I didn't know how to get home.

As I was thinking about escaping school, the word "Lunch" came to mind. I wanted it to be lunchtime so badly that, when there were only five minutes left of class, I was already packed and ready. I nearly had one foot out the door.

I was looking forward to lunch because my cousins were attending the same school, which meant I would know people who understood my language and knew me. My cousins would be friends I could hold on to. And, also, I was hungry. As usual, I wanted to eat!

Lunchtime finally came. As planned, for thirty minutes straight, I sat next to my cousins as if I were their well-trained dog. I didn't want them to escape my sight, much less my orbit. I was like a leech. I stuck to them without letting go. As soon as the bell announced lunch was over, I started walking to my next class: Math. My sight was fixated on the gray tile. I didn't even want to make eye contact with anyone.

But when I entered my math class, I immediately entered a harmonious space. I had reached my comfort zone! I didn't need to know English in Math. The numbers in Spanish were the same as in English. And in this class, I didn't need to present myself, because nobody cared about the new kid. I just needed to know how to multiply and add, so everything was going to go smoothly.

Two hours of math were relaxing. I sat at the back of the room and took notes for the entire duration of the class without looking at others. I made up stories in my head, and asked myself questions: Will I eat a hamburger for dinner? Is my mom going to forget to pick me up?

My concentration on the math problems, my calculator and my thoughts led me, for a tiny bit, to forget the fact that I was new. Math sort of made me fly to another worry-free dimension, in which I was able to breathe without feeling like an alien. In fewer, simpler words, I was in my own little world!

Finally, the day was over. Before leaving, I copied down the homework assignments. "Thank you, God!" I wrote under the homework. I had gone through my first day of school without crying in the bathroom—as I had when I'd attended kindergarten for the first time—or running away, although I had crapped my pants a bit! In general, it was an okay day.

The next few months were similar to my first day of school. Eventually, I started talking to some people, just making normal conversation. Did I make new friends? Not really. I never saw most of those kids after my first semester. Summer began, and I was transferred to another school. In a matter of six months, I had fled the "new kid" zone. But then I had to become the new kid all over again.

New school, new challenges, new people, new ideas. That is how I started my seventh grade. Summer had been calm. I had spent the summer at my house, eating and watching television. From time to time, I saw my cousins. Yet again, I had entered a new territory. This time, the territory was bigger. Older people. Gloomier classrooms. Far from welcoming. The cool people on one side and the cute girls in another. The cheerleaders conquering the cafeteria. The football players making a mockery out of everyone else's pitiful lives. Teachers whistling everywhere. Baseball players, just like dogs, pissing everywhere to mark their territory.

And then, there I was, standing in the middle of all of this hubbub without knowing what to do. I felt as awkward as a kid possibly could. Once more, in a couple of hours at that new school, all my demons had entered me: fear, embarrassment, etc.

The first few days were brutal, just like my first days at my old school. Being unknown and feeling unknown, sitting at a red lunchroom table by myself or just pretending to walk around school, acting like I had things to do—that's how I spent my first few pitiful lunches. My English had not improved much, and neither had my courage to talk to others. I knew I had to find my comfort zone, a place where I would be able to develop as a happy human being and feel satisfied with myself.

That's what I did . . . sort of.

Every day after school, I could see young teens my age hanging out with their friends. They would walk down the street with their posses. Some kids were going to each other's houses, or even heading to the movies. They seemed normal, and I felt like an outcast. While they were acting like young teens, I was in my own little world.

I was very vulnerable. I was trying to adapt to a new way of living and my old enemy, Obesity, took advantage. He knew how to hypnotize me into believing that food and television could alleviate all my discomfort.

I became addicted to food—unhealthy food! I couldn't live a minute without food. In front of the television, I needed to have something to eat, from ice cream to fried chicken. When I was bored, I had to have food, from chocolate to pizza. As I was doing homework, I needed food, from buttery popcorn to spicy Cheetos. Before going to sleep, I needed a snack, from Oreo cookies to a bowl of Cocoa Puffs. When I woke up, I needed food, from refried beans to fried eggs.

My addiction escorted me to a point where I couldn't act normal without having food, to a point where I couldn't function. My self-esteem was already at the ground level. I thought it couldn't go below zero, but food made that possible. I don't mean "good" food, I mean sundaes, french fries, burgers with

bacon and American cheese, chocolate and ice cream, chocolate fudge, chips, sodas, etc. Even though I was so low down,
alone and depressed, Obesity wanted even more. He wanted to
go the extra mile.

Television, just like food, held me back, and I don't mean
only physically. It held me back psychologically, too. I had literally been raised as a savage, in a cave. I wasn't able to, and
didn't know how to, socialize. I had lost sense of the word
"friends" and even of the word "people." I didn't know how to
act with others—just saying a simple "Hi" became a challenge—
since I was always sitting in the living room and living in a fantasy land with only one resident: me. In my fantasy land, I felt
welcome. Unhealthy *Bert-Land!*

I could sit for more than six hours in front of the television,
with food on hand, and not even blink. I would sit as close to
the set as possible, so close that I could smell the characters'
sweat. My shoulders slouched down and my back became
hunched. My face would go blank and I would enter another
dimension. I couldn't live without TV. It was part of my daily
routine; television and snacks, both, became me.

My cousins would come to visit me and try to talk to me,
but instead of saying "Hi," I would press my index finger over
my lips and "shhhh" them. Right after the "shhhh" moment, I
would welcome them to watch television and eat. I didn't know
anything else.

When I would try to stand up from the sofa and leave the
house, Food and Television would stretch their hands out and
pull me back. They weren't letting go, and I wasn't really trying
to escape. They were strong and I was weak, mentally and physically. I wasn't fighting. I was tired and frustrated with my new
life and I wanted to escape. I had become something like a drug
addict. With Food and Television I felt understood, accompanied and protected. I felt that they knew where I was coming
from and what I needed. They were always next to me when-

ever I needed them. I didn't have to beg for their friendship; I just had to be me. They did not judge me or put me down. It felt as if they were protecting me from the cruelty outside.

Most of the time, my parents were working. Immigrating to a new country demanded that they work night and day. They had to build a new household from scratch. They had to find new ways to support the household. They were trying to build our new life while Obesity was working on tearing it down.

Because I was alone most of the time, Television and Food—and Obesity—were destroying me, little by little. And of course, my parents were unaware of this situation. Even if I had known what was going on, I wouldn't have had betrayed my only friends.

I, truly and innocently, thought Food and Television had given me the tranquility and happiness I needed. But they never really cared about me. They were in alliance with Obesity. Obesity had used them to get me to the point where he wanted me to be: self-destruction. With cold hits, they were destroying me, and I wasn't even fighting back. Was the war being lost, or had it been lost already?

Chapter 8

My Body Is Taken Over
September 12, 2003

You're so fat, you had to be baptized at Water World....
You're so fat, Fat Ass! ... Are you hungry all the time? ...
You're so fat that, when you step on a scale, it says, "One
at a time, PLEASE!" ... You're so fat, you sweat corn oil....
You're so fat, you rented a 250-foot long limo, sat in the
back and squished the poor driver! ...

IT WAS MY TWELFTH BIRTHDAY AND NOW WE WERE IN A NEW
country, starting from zero, so my extravagant parties were over.
Now it was just us and my dad's family. My twelfth was going to
be the smallest birthday party I had ever had. There were only
about fifteen people and, probably, most of them didn't even
care that it was my birthday. Some came early and left early;
some came late and left early.

The party was another sign that told me I wasn't welcome
here and that I was very different from everyone else. I missed
my family back home, and I wished they could have been with
me.

Back in San Salvador, the 2003 party would have been the
Pokémon year; all of the Pokémons would have been hung from
the ceiling and my cake would have been decorated with them.
But now, I only had some balloons hanging from the ceiling and

my cake was an average, store-bought one, with some balloons drawn on it and a "Happy Birthday, Alberto."

I knew I couldn't spend the entire party thinking about what would have occurred back home. I had to change my train of thought, appreciate what I had, and make the best of it. I had to show appreciation for what my mom had done. As soon as I saw the burgers and cake, my frown turned upside down. Those were true friends, I thought. We had just sat down when my stomach began growling. Then, my mom announced, "Dinner's ready!" My cousins and I jumped off the sofa and immediately began fast-walking toward the kitchen and getting in line, with our plates in front us. I was at the end of the line, drooling over my future hamburger.

When I finally got to the front of the line, one of my aunts was waiting with a very juicy burger in her hands, one that was calling my name: "Alberto, come get me! I'm here!" I placed the plate right under her hands and the hamburger dropped onto it, along with some fries. I was also handed a glass full of soda to accompany them. Obviously, my eyes were pinwheels of joy!

We walked back to the living room, sat down on the couch, and watched my favorite TV show: Pokémon. Dinner was quiet. Nobody talked; we only chewed and drank. Instead of having the "Happy Birthday" song as the background music, we had "Pikachu come back" and "Charmander attack!" We were so mesmerized by the show that an elephant could have walked through the room and we wouldn't have even noticed.

In a matter of minutes, I jumped off the couch and headed back to the kitchen, with my cousin following me.

"Seconds, please," we said simultaneously. The adults didn't say anything. We didn't have to trick them or hide our second helpings. They grabbed more burgers and placed them on our plates. "Fries?" one of my aunts asked. My cousin said "No, thanks" but I said "Yes!" I knew my mom wasn't happy about how much I was eating, but she couldn't do anything about it.

If she said something, my dad's family would have eaten her alive; they were—and are—anti-healthy. So even if my mom had fought them, she would have lost. Again, we took our plates and went back to the living room. We sat, ate and watched TV. Those were our only activities at my birthday party! When we were done eating and the show was over, it was cake time! The adults put a small, portable table in the middle of the living room and sat the cake on it. As my mom was lighting my twelve candles, Marcela, one of my cousins, was turning off the lights to make the singing more dramatic. I knelt in front of the cake, as if I were in church, and was about to pray to my God when they began singing. I really didn't care about their singing, and not only because they were terrible. I merely wanted to dive into the cake and eat it all!

As soon as they stopped singing and the lights were turned on, I dipped my index finger into the cake and grabbed some frosting. I brought my finger to my mouth and I smiled. Another sugar high! It was so good that I dipped my finger in again before they took the cake into the kitchen and began to cut it up.

We had to wait for a few minutes before we were called into the kitchen. Once more, the first to jump off of the couch and head to the waiting line were my cousin and I. The cake had been cut up and all the pieces lay on plates on the table. We were going to choose the piece we wanted!

I examined the table: I wanted the biggest one. I stretched my arm out and grabbed it. Merrily, I walked back to the living room, sat down on the couch and stared at the TV again. The cake gave me the greatest sugar high I had ever experienced. My palate had been introduced to a new and indescribable sugar level. My face was kissing the plate and all the frosting and crumbs were hanging from my lips. I ate like I was afraid that cake was my last meal! Less than three minutes had gone by, and I was already pushing myself up from the couch again. I fast-walked back to the kitchen and grabbed another piece.

This time, I didn't want to push it; a thinner slice was perfect. As soon as I was done with the second piece, the party was over. It was about 10 p.m. and we had to go get ready for the next day: Pool Day!

Pool Day was one of the presents I had asked my parents for. I have always loved swimming, but as we were trying to adapt to a new life, I forgot about it. That day marked my return to the water. I was so excited that I went to buy new trunks and a white T-shirt with Hawaiian Flowers on it. I felt as if I had won a gold medal at the Olympics and I was returning to my country to show it off.

The pool where my parents took my two cousins and me was about five blocks away from my house. It was a community pool, located in the middle of a park. As always, we drove to our final destination, even though it was close enough to walk there. Unluckily, the American traffic situation had turned into a Salvadoran one. It took us twenty minutes to get there.

Anyway, we finally arrived just before noon. The benches surrounding the two pools and the pools themselves were crowded with people. There were two pools: one for kids and another for adults, much like the Spanish Country Club. Kids were running up and down; lifeguards were whistling and following them with their red noodles, trying to stop them; and parents were screaming at the kids to be careful.

As soon as I saw all that chaos, I froze. It was not what I had expected. Thankfully, we were able to find a piece of bench where we could land our butts. But to get to that piece of bench, we had to cross the entire arena. I knew everyone was looking at us. I could feel their staring eyes, although I couldn't see them because my own eyes were fixated on the gray, wet ground.

As we were settling down, embarrassment welled up in me. I saw shirtless boys and men swimming back and forth. Some were playing, some were showing off their muscles, and others were flirting. It was a mix of everything that afternoon, but I didn't belong to that mix. A bulging Curly couldn't be hanging around the "cool" people.

"Go in!" my mom yelled at me once I stood at pool's edge. I didn't even bother to look back. There were some kids awaiting my jump, while others were trying to swim as fast as possible so I wouldn't land on them. I didn't want to go into the water, especially if I was going to be the only one wearing a T-shirt. As I was thinking about quitting, I felt two hands and pressure on my back. My cousin, Rolando, had pushed me. I plopped under the water and surfaced. Then Rolando splashed in right next to me.

Maybe my panicked voice had been screaming inside of me as I was looking at the shirtless kids, but once I was in the water, everything calmed down. We swam and played in the water for two hours until they opened the trampoline. Simultaneously, all the lifeguards whistled a shrill sound that resonated in every single ear. The arena became so quiet that a pin drop could be heard. Someone with a megaphone declared, "Trampoline open until four o'clock."

I looked at my cousin and we were of one mind. We hurried to the trampoline and got in line. There were about ten people in front of us, and they were clearly taking their time. It made for a miserable wait. Some were showing off their moves and muscles, others were crying and quitting, and others were still flirting . . . I don't know how they were managing to jump and flirt at the same time, but they were. Crazies!

As my turn was coming up, I felt a finger touching my shoulder. It was one of those firm fingers that feels like it's about to make a hole. I turned around and saw a lifeguard with a disgusting face standing behind me.

"No shirt!" he warned out loud.

As he finished screaming "NO shirt!" for the third time, I snapped out of my daydream and found that everybody was staring at me. It was my turn, but before I could go on the trampoline, I had to take off my shirt.

I became as red as the red noodle the lifeguard was holding. I didn't want to take off my shirt. I wanted to scream at him that I couldn't. Everybody was muscular, lean and thin, and I didn't want to become the creepy kid.

A year had flown by since we had moved to California, and my stomach had grown into a tire. And I don't mean just any tire; I mean a 4 X 4 truck tire. My belly was so big that I was wearing size 36 pants and size Large shirts. I had skipped my early youth, jumping from children's clothes to adult clothes in matter of months. On top of it all, my belly wasn't rigid: it was as flaccid and squishy as a bag filled with pudding and gelatin. With every step I took, it jiggled and looked deformed. It was hanging so much that it covered up my belt buckle. It had outgrown me.

My belly was so big that it had begun to stretch my skin. Every day, more stretch marks appeared. First, they started on the front of my belly, and then they moved and began to appear on the sides. Once my belly had no more space, they started to move upwards. The sides of my torso were full of stretch marks; my arms began to be covered with them, too. My old-man boobs also had grown so they looked as if they could have exploded like water balloons during one of my birthday parties. Stretch marks had also appeared around my nipples, making them look like cracked chocolate cookies.

Obesity had been acting like an ancient, cannibalistic dog, peeing in every corner of my body, marking its territory. I was full of those marks and I didn't want to be a spectacle. I didn't want to take off my shirt in front of everybody and let them see my body.

Because of my increasing size, my self-esteem had left the building a long time ago. As I was standing in front of the trampoline and wondering whether to take my shirt off, I learned something I had never realized. It was something nobody should even think about. At that moment, with the lifeguard standing right in front of me, and everybody's eyes locked on me, I learned to hate myself.

I hated Curly: Alberto Hidalgo-Robert. I hated every single bit of me. I hated the bulge hanging over my belt. I was disgusted with my body. My stretch marks had become the signature of my self-hate.

In simple words, I was malformed. I was hideous, revolting, nasty and ghastly, and my only wish at that instant was to evaporate. To magically disappear. To use my Pokémon and fly away and never come back. To twitch my nose and fade away. To become Harry Potter, use my magic wand and vanish. One, two, three . . . nothing!

Sadly, *abracadabra*—or any other mantra I was reciting in my head—wasn't going to work.

My bulge and my stretch marks weren't going anywhere. Taking my shirt off wasn't even an option. I was under no illusion. That idea came with a big, black and white "NO." It was written in stone and signed with my fat, self-hating blood: "So Not Going to Happen!"

I opted to quit, to bail on myself, again. I walked out of the line and headed to the bench. As I left, everyone saw me. My walk showed my defeat: my head was bowed down, and I was feeling embarrassed, like a failure.

As I sat, my mom asked me what was going on. I told her, "Let's go. My favorite show's going to start."

I learned that hibernating at home and covering up with big, baggy jackets and sweaters or colorful shirts would take the attention of off me, those were the only ways out of this constant embarrassment. I made myself invisible. My clothes were my armor, protecting me from the scrutiny of others. Obesity had managed not only to ruin my social life, he had managed to put the seed of self-hate within me, right inside my heart. My self-confidence was destroyed, shattered into millions of Bert pieces. I wasn't able to walk in front of people without feeling out of place. It was as if I wore a red flag at all times. I felt that people were terrified of coming near me. I felt I was like herpes, disgusting and contaminating. I was an ailment and people didn't want to catch it.

The episode at the pool taught me two things. First, that I wouldn't be able to cover myself for the rest of my life. Second, I wasn't going to be able to disappear.

This time, Obesity had done it. He had lowered my self-esteem and confidence below the ground; now I felt inferior. Obesity had destroyed my life. He had won the war completely. At that point, I had given up; my parents had given up. There was nothing else to do except put my future, my life and everything I had, into his hands. He had taken my childhood, my early youth   and my life, just as my stretch marks had taken over my body . . . for the rest of my life.

Chapter 9

"Pants Off, Fat Ass"
2004

I JUST WANTED TO BE NORMAL, LIKE EVERYBODY ELSE, TO FIT IN. Everyone seemed to have an advantage over Curly: physically, romantically and in every other aspect you can think of . . . except academically. Math, social studies, art and science classes were my areas of expertise. I was always fond of adding and subtracting, fascinated by how the planet was created and by European history, how our bodies work and how to make a turtle out of paper maché. I loved, and still love, making my brain work, making it run as if it was in a race. I liked making my brain think until my head hurt, my eyes burned and until I could understand new ideas.

But in middle school, there was one problem: I was the "fat-ass nerd." Even though I was at the top of the class academically, always getting A's, nobody respected me. All of my classmates were fond of sports, and there I had the biggest disadvantage. Ever since the age of four, my parents had been pushing me into playing sports, even though I didn't like any of them: not karate, not soccer, not basketball, not baseball and definitely not football. I never learned to kick, dribble, bat or throw a ball. I was more into books. I was more into writing and drawing than running and kicking. I was more into learning and thinking than sweating and swinging.

I can sit and watch a few games and cheer for a team. But I was never attracted to play any sport, because I knew I would be the weight holding the team down. I was always the team member who wouldn't move as fast as the others or the one who was too shy to tackle someone.

I remember during fifth grade, when I was still living in El Salvador, my parents had decided to sign me up for a basketball team, because my dad had been a basketball player, and they wanted me to be like him. Once more, I went with the flow and did as they said—what else could I do?—and I put the blue jersey and shorts on and I tied my basketball shoes. I got on the court and made a fool out of myself for the first few games. In one word, I was horrible. I would lose the ball the most easily. I wasn't able to run fast or score a point, and I had to deal with my belly and my uncontrollable sweating. Every time I ran, I could feel my belly jogging with me. It wasn't stable; it was so fleshy, I thought it was going to rip away from my body and fall on the court. Every time I would land on one foot, I could feel gravity pulling my belly down. And every time I would move, my sweaty jersey would show the real size of my belly.

By the third game, I hated every minute. I hated my jersey and shorts, I hated my parents and I really hated my belly. By the fourth game, my frustration and my belly got the best of me. "I get tired too quickly and I don't like it," I told my parents as I was hanging my jersey on the doorknob of their room. I was quitting, once again. Every time I did something I didn't like and it didn't feel comfortable, I would quit.

I had many experiences like that basketball incident, but with different sports, up until my twelfth year of life. I remember, in eighth grade, we used to run "the mile," a dreadful and painful weekly race of four laps around the baseball field. We were supposed to try to run it in under twelve minutes, although for me, it took more than nineteen minutes. I put effort into it, but there was a problem: that tire-like lump of meat around me. Trying to move an extra twenty pounds wasn't easy. I couldn't breathe, and I would end up gasping like a dying fish out of water.

It was impossible for me to move a lump of fleshy meat for four laps, nonstop. On top of all that, my so-called "friends" —if you can call them that—would use my misery as an opportunity for mockery. They would push me around or call me names as I tried to run. When I was done, they would call my time out loud and make fun of my slothfulness. I would walk away head down, closed mouth and breathing heavily.

But there was way more than name calling, pushing and mocking. Everything would start in the locker room. "Ten minutes to change into your gym clothes!" the coach would yell after blowing his whistle. In a matter of seconds, shorts were flying, shirts were taken off, muscle shows began and the awful smell of sweat would invade my nostrils. There I'd be in the corner, trying to change into my pants while hiding my flab.

"Fat-ass!" one of those "cool" kids would call out. "You're not a man!" They implied I should stop hiding, show everything off, and be a man. My face would get red and the entire locker room would grow quiet. I was being put on the spot; the only way to escape was to pretend I was getting a text message. I would grab my phone and pretend I was typing. The "cool" kid would just laugh at me—I bet he was thinking how pathetic I was—and the whole locker-room scene would continue: jokes and laughs thrown around, muscle shows and kids whipping each other with their T-shirts.

Changing my shirt was the worst of it: I didn't want anyone to see my stretch marks. I'd try to change into my gym shirt without taking my regular shirt off by slipping my gym shirt over and then removing my regular shirt from underneath, all the while trying not to show anything. It was comical, but painful! I didn't want to show my stretch marks, or the spilling fat over the waistband of my jeans, because I knew gossip would get around every corner of the school.

One Thursday, everything took a turn for the worse. While we were waiting for the whistle to announce the start of the race, we crammed together at the starting line. The "cool" kid who used to bug me in the locker room was right behind me. I could feel his eyes boring into my back. Suddenly, I felt a warm breath—which smelled like chips—blowing by my ear. "You gonna show now," he said to me. As I was trying to ignore him, I felt a gush of air on my legs.

Suddenly, guys were pointing at me and calling me "fat-ass geek." Some were calling out, "Stop eating!" I realized with horror that my loose tire, my turkey thighs and my fat ass were exposed for the world to see. I had been "pantsed." The "cool" guys had taken to pulling other guys' pants down, especially guys like me, guys who were vulnerable and different. And by "different" I mean guys with man boobs and fat asses, guys who were not willing to fight or even open their mouths, guys who were book buddies or "teachers' pets."

I was so embarrassed, standing there outside in my underwear for the entire world to see. I remember, so vividly, bending down to pull my pants up. While I was down there, in between my legs, I caught a glimpse of kids pointing at my butt and pretending it was a target. My face turned red; even my ears were burning. I had gone through the worst moment of my life, right in front of everyone!

What could I do? Nothing! I had to pick my pants and my head up and act like my normal self. I had to pretend nothing had happened. I remember this girl came up to me and asked me if I was all right. I really don't know how deformed my face was, but I must have scared her. She ran away without waiting for an answer.

I wanted to run away, too, but I didn't have anywhere to go. I wanted to hide, but I didn't have any place to do so. I wanted to scream, but I was speechless. I didn't have any way out. I had to swallow what had just happened and continue. I was breaking down on the inside, but showing my emotions wasn't an option. I couldn't complain to the teacher or my parents, because that would also make me a "fat-ass sissy geek." I couldn't defend myself, physically, because I didn't even know how to kick or punch.

I started running the mile. What else was I supposed to do? An assignment was an assignment. And even a fat-ass geek like me wasn't going to fail a school assignment.

As I was finishing my last lap, I started looking for my coach, because I had to report my time. When I stopped at the finish line, he wasn't there. He had gotten weary, exasperated by my podgy-turtle run—a run that, every now and then, would last more than twenty minutes. Today, I can still imagine my coach at the end point of our mile, tapping his foot, slamming shut his red little notebook where he kept the record of our times. I can imagine him scratching his gray-haired head, feeling his ever-present sweat rolling down his cheeks as he bit his nails to the quick. I bet it was torture for him to wait, but it was more torture for me to look halfway down the track and see nobody waiting for me. He wasn't cheering me on, or even screaming "Let's go, lazy a-s-s-s-s-s!"

In the end, what I got out of this was that everything was my fault. I was holding everybody back: my coach, my class, myself. That was part of the price I had to pay for my plumpness and slowness: not having anyone wait at the finish line, to see my blubber bouncing up and down.

My coach, with the rest of my class, would just go sit in the locker room and wait for me to come and announce that I was done so they could leave for lunch. Other times, he would stop me at the third lap and say "Okay, we all know you're gonna make it in nineteen, so go ahead and stop." I never accomplished my twelve-minute-mile goal during middle school. That assignment became one of the things I feared the most.

The day of my "pantsing," after I had finished running, I was walking toward the locker room to change into my street clothes, when someone called me a "pussy." Someone else asked me why I didn't do anything to defend myself. Others kept laughing and asked me if I was hungry. Once again, I walked to my corner of the locker room and started changing: showing no ass, no man boobs, no tire-like belly, no stretch marks, no nothing! This time, it took me less than five minutes to step out of that locker room. The locker room, running track and those kids were added to my "Hate" list. And I also hated myself even more for not defending myself. I felt ostracized by everyone. Obesity had managed to make me outgrow everyone (you know what I mean), and everybody was laughing about it. Obesity had managed to convert me into an easy target, with a "Hit Me, I'm Not Moving" sign right in the middle of my back.

Chapter 10

Fat in the Homeland
December 2005-January 3, 2006

APPROXIMATELY TWO MONTHS AFTER MY FOURTEENTH BIRTHDAY, I got the greatest gift I had ever received. We were going back home. My mom handed me an envelope, looked me straight in the eyes and said, "I love you, and this is from both of us." My hands were shaking, I was so very nervous to see what the envelope contained. I sat down at the dining room table. The first words I saw were the name of the airline. Under the airline's name was my name, and under my name was my seat number and the date we were leaving. We are going to El Salvador for Christmas! I was going to see my cousins, my aunts and uncles, and, of course, my grandmother and my dog.

On December 15, 2005, when the plane landed in San Salvador, I felt the same sensation I had felt when the plane had landed in San Francisco two years earlier. My entire body began sweating and became covered in goose bumps. I couldn't believe it! I was back to my roots, back to the place where El Gordito was born and Curly had evolved. I knew my cousins were waiting for us outside, with Uncle Atto and my grandmother beside them. It took twenty minutes to clear customs. The automatic doors opened and the morning sun was shining on us. It warmed my heart once again. I was, truly, back home! Then I caught a glimpse of two Asian-looking kids waving their hands above their heads. A good-looking grandmother stood next to them. "Welcome, Gordito!" my grandmother said, pulling me toward her for a hug.

This hug was very different from the good-bye hug she had given me two years earlier. Back then, she was able to wrap her arms around me and squish the hell out of me, but this time I was too big for her to reach around.

My cousins were giving me a weird stare, looking me up and down. When a dog barked, they awoke from their thoughts and jumped on me and gave me a hug. Next to them was Uncle Atto. As soon as I heard him call me "Curly," I knew I was back home. Curly was back!

As the garage door opened that morning, fireworks went off: our welcome. My aunts, Lorena and Betty, stood at the door with my Nana behind them. Diego, the youngest of my three cousins, stood in front of my aunts, and Negra, my French poodle, was running around. This was exactly what I needed: people who loved me. Here, I didn't feel repulsive. Instead, my expectations were reached and surpassed. My welcome back home was perfect. It felt just as if I were receiving a big, warm hug from the entire country.

We got out of the car, and hugs and kisses were given everywhere, but there were some weird looks. My relatives eyes were bugging out, but I immediately disregarded them, because I was too captivated by my exciting return. I was also mesmerized by the refried beans and fried eggs waiting for me at the table.

Our first few days were exquisite. I was enjoying Salvadoran *quesadillas*, *pupusas*, *tamales*, Fried chicken and sweet bread.

Before Santa Claus came to town, we had a big get-together. What better place to celebrate than the country club? It was not the "most amazing" place (that was the beach house!), but it was *the* better place. The country club looked just the same. The pools were in the same place; the bar, where I had gotten my second burger during my eighth birthday party, was still standing; the outdoor rooms were in the same spots, but they had been upgraded. Everything was familiar, and I liked it. Here, I knew where everything was. I wasn't a stranger.

My mom and aunts sat down while my cousins and I admired the pool, as if it were a lost treasure. We were so excited that they immediately took their shirts off and their mothers began to rub sunblock onto their tiny backs and faces. I was just waiting for them, sitting down, eating some courtesy chips and wearing my trunks and my yellow, Size X-Large T-shirt.

We ran to the pool as fast as we could. Flash! A picture was taken. My cousins, three years younger than me, were sitting next to me. I felt like a star, and believe me, that picture was an attention-grabber. My mom, who had snapped the picture, went back and showed it to my aunts. As she was showing it, Uncle Raúl came up to her and welcomed her home.

My mom reciprocated the love, hugs and kisses. Uncle Raúl asked for me, but at that time I was swimming and I didn't want to come out; I was having too much fun. Instead of calling me out of the pool, my mom showed Uncle Raúl the picture she had just taken. She said later that, the instant he got a look at the picture, his mouth dropped open and his eyes widened as if they were about to pop!

"Chila, he's so big!" he told my mother. "He's obese. You need to take care of him. He's too young to be that big. Look at his cousins. He looks like at least five years older than they are, and they're, only three years apart!"

Thank God the rest of family arrived just then, ending the embarrassing episode for my mom. It would've been the most awkward lunch of my entire vacation if my uncle had kept bombarding my mom with comments about my weight!

That same night, after the get-together at the Country Club, a "Welcome" jamboree was to take place at my grandparent's home. The most pivotal one: *My Big Fat Salvadoran Dinner.*

To get ready for our guests, we swept the floor, dusted off the windows, lit candles, prepared chips and sodas and moved furniture so more people could fit. A chicken was baked and rice was cooked. We also bought fireworks. Fireworks, we felt, were the quintessential way to say, "The family is back together!"

My parents and I took showers and dressed in our best clothes. I dressed in a dark blue, plain polo shirt and light jeans, with a brown belt and brown shoes. I was going to present myself in front of everybody, for the first time in three years.

As everyone started arriving, I quickly ran into in the bathroom, splashed on some cologne and checked my hair. The one thing I didn't check was my outfit.

I tried to make a big entrance. As I walked through the hallway, I started to hear their voices. As I got closer, the murmurs and then the laughter and giggles grew louder. By then, I had already identified everyone who was waiting for me; in a matter of seconds, I remembered everybody's voices.

As I entered and said "Hello," their faces paled and eyes popped. The silence was unbearable! Finally, some of them unfroze and forced smiles. Others just kept staring.

Ironically, I did make a BIG entrance, but not the one I had planned.

It was a bit agonizing at first, not being welcomed back. But then, suddenly, everyone rapidly jumped up from their seats and started kissing and hugging me. Uncle César shook my hand and then he gave me a hug. He leaned toward me and began tapping my tummy—of course, it was jiggling—as he said, "Gotta exercise!" Those two words expressed what the rest of the crowd was thinking. My bulging fat was the center of attention. I had fought for three years to hide and ignore my corpulence. But now I was back home, where everybody—supposedly—loved me, and the first thing they noticed was my protruding fat.

How could I have not noticed it? My outfit was still Curly's: my shirt was tightly stretched over my overflowing belly and man-boobs. My double chin was touching my shirt's collar and hiding my collarbone. Because the shirt had short sleeves, my stretch-marked, flabby, sausage arms were clearly visible. My size 38 pants were hugging my blubbery legs, and my belt buckle was hidden behind my drooping belly.

My brown shoes were packaging my big, fat tamale-feet. Earlier that evening, I realized that tying my shoelaces was impossible, since catching my breath had become a struggle. Consequently, my laces were only tucked into the sides of the shoes.

To top it all, because of the humid weather, a drop of sweat was rolling down my forehead onto my neck and my double chin. My abhorrent fat was melting!

When my relatives saw me, it was as if they had just seen a ghost or some unrecognizable entity. Their faces seemed lost and blank.

Later that evening, I glanced over at the dinner table, and I saw my mom and my dad sitting down with my uncles and aunts. I am pretty nosy, but that time, I knew I couldn't go over to them. I had to stay out and pretend they were not gossiping about me, even though my mom and dad would turn around, every minute or so, to look at me. I knew they were saying my name, and it was not in a favorable context. The party continued until midnight, when everybody started getting ready to leave. While they were saying their good-byes, I quietly leaned over to my mom, pulled her down to my level and asked her what everyone had been talking about. She immediately hugged me, which entirely shut me up and whisked my question away along with the fumes coming from the departing cars. I knew she didn't want to talk about it. The outcome of that discussion, I later found out, was to take place back in San Francisco. It wasn't until we were back in California that the eerie looks and talks were explained to me.

Soon after returning from our Salvadoran trip, my mom demanded—she didn't ask, she d.e.m.a.n.d.e.d—that I go to the pediatrician. She wasn't kidding. She turned the television off and took my plate of food away. This was serious matter! She sat me down, right after she came home from work, and gave me the facts, nonstop: "We're going to the appointment on the tenth, and that is my final decision. It's going to be Tuesday at nine a.m., and you must be fasting. We don't know if you'll have to take some blood tests, so we have to go prepared. Okay? We'll leave at eight-thirty."

After the kicking, screaming and crying for ten minutes straight, was I off the hook? "No! You are going, and this conversation is over!" said my mom as she banged a wooden spoon on the stove.

It turns out my parents had found a specialist in obesity. They were set to take me to Thomas Robinson, MD, MPH, Director of the Center for Healthy Weight at Lucile Packard Children's Hospital at Stanford.

"We need to know that you're in good shape. We want to know if you're healthy," my parents told me after they had sat me down on the couch. "No! I'm not going! Especially if he has to do with nutrition and all that stuff . . . he'll only give me more diets. That's what the other doctor did." How could I really soften their hearts? I had to do something soap opera-ish. I had to make an impact to change the already-made plans. "The nutritionists are all the same," I began. "They're just going to test me again with the stupid diets. If a nutritionist is checking me, I won't go." The pitch of my voice was rising, and to add a bit more spice to my pitiful melodrama, I screamed at my mom and dad, "I don't trust them. I'm just an experiment for them. And I'm tired!" I ran to my room and slammed the door behind me. I thought I had them eating from my hand. I really thought my act was going to pay off and I was waiting for them to say, "We're sorry, you don't have to go." I was standing behind the door with my ear stuck to it, extremely sure I had won.

No response came from the other side of the door! They could have agreed with me, since they knew how much I had suffered back home due to the cruel and constraining diets I had tried. But this time, they didn't seem to care if I cried or screamed or broke anything, or even if there was an earthquake or a thunderstorm. They were worried about me, and they just wanted to make sure I was healthy. They weren't taking chances anymore.

I was set against going to Dr. Robinson, but they knew why this change had to occur. My parents had seen how our family in El Salvador reacted to the way I looked and acted. As a consequence, they had realized there was something wrong—not only with me, but with our way of living. Something that we were unable to grasp, and somehow we had let it go too far.

That had been the first "wake-up call." That conversation with my family had opened their eyes, just a bit, and now they were looking through a keyhole into reality: a small ray of light at the end of the dark tunnel we had chosen to live in. Worries about my health had been bothering them, and my mother had decided to stop them. The only way she knew to do this was by making me go to a doctor, a specialist in what obviously ailed me.

"Hello, I'm here for my appointment," I said as I made an I-don't-like-you face to the receptionist. I was standing on my tippy toes in front of a white counter at the Lucile Packard Children's Hospital and searching with the palm of my hand for the candy basket I was used to. She asked for my name and my age. "Alberto Hidalgo, and I'm thirteen," I said.

"We need your mom to sign this paperwork," she told me. I called my mom, and she walked over and filled out the paperwork. Then we sat down in the waiting area. In less than ten minutes, a nurse was calling me in. Again, in just a matter of seconds—exactly the way it happened back home—I was standing on a gray, electronic scale. The nightmare I dreaded the most had once again become a reality. The numbers started rolling by. Ninety pounds.

One hundred.

One hundred and fifty.

One hundred and eighty-five.

Stop!

I held my head up and stopped looking at the changing numbers. I pretended I knew my weight and didn't need to know it again. Next, my height. I stood up straight, with my back facing the wall, feet together and looked straight up. I was five feet and eight inches. That measurement mattered a lot to me. I felt like an adult since I was growing taller.

Despite all of my intimidating measurements, the nurse asked my age, once again, and escorted me to my room. I sat by myself for, let's say, thirty seconds. Then a knock disturbed my peace.

"Come in!" I said. He entered, shook my hand and presented himself, as I stood up to present myself. "Hi, I'm Doctor Robinson, your new pediatrician," he said, adding, "*and* nutrition specialist."

I smiled and sat right back down. I didn't introduce myself after he added the nutrition part. I wanted to show him that I was so disinterested in nutrition, saying my name became pointless. I was so hesitant to talk about my diet that becoming a bitchy, obnoxious, snotty kid was in order. I didn't speak for the first five minutes. I pretended not to listen. On top of everything else, I started chewing my nails and getting out the dirt under them.

He continued talking and talking and trying and trying. He began explaining food, exercise and obesity . . .

Wait! Obesity? As soon as he mentioned the O-word, my owl-like eyes opened, my brain started working as if it were machinery in a factory, fuming at the top. I started listening . . .

Dr. Robinson showed me a chart with two curved lines (the Weight-Percentile Curves or, in non-medical terms, growth charts). "The red one is you," he said as I smiled. The red curve was way at the top.

"Your BMI is thirty-two," he told me. "The red curve represents that." Then he began explaining "Body Mass Index." It's the ratio of someone's body weight and height (weight divided by height). The highest BMI is 40, which is Obesity Stage III; BMI 37 is the top end of Stage II; BMI 32 is the top of Stage I. A healthy measurement is a BMI of 22.

I got keyed up! Mine was thirty-two and that meant I was close to forty, the highest BMI!

The doctor was not sure I was getting the point of the talk; it was as if he were talking to Humpty Dumpty. I was sitting there with my eyes wide open, my hands idiotically scratching my head. So he escorted me to the waiting area, where my mom was waiting, and told me to wait out there while he spoke with my mom. She stood up and followed him. Back in the examining room, he told her, "This is his weight." The three digits she saw were disturbing, and the BMI chart was horrifying. The last time she had seen this chart was when I was ten and we were still living in El Salvador. My ex-pediatrician had shown it to her, but he hadn't explained anything. At that time, I had been fixated on the lollipop he'd given me, so even if he had explained it, I never heard!

This time, the 32 BMI and my weight had become Wake-up Call Número Dos. After realizing what was going on and almost crying, my mother told Dr. Robinson, "I didn't realize he was that big."

She said he replied, "Do you notice the lamp you have in your living room every day?"

Confused, she'd answered, "No. . ."

"Exactly," the doctor said. "Alberto is like that lamp. You are so used to seeing him every day that a slow, yet colossal, change, such as this one, is unrecognizable. It's just like a plant in your house. You water and fertilize it every day, but you're so used to seeing that plant that you never notice its growth until someone brings it to your attention." In my case, the plant was overwatered!

He was correct. My change hadn't happened overnight. My change had been a snail and had taken more than a decade. Only the people who saw me once in a while were able to notice and comment on it. That was exactly what had occurred with my relatives back in El Salvador. They hadn't seen me for two years, so when they saw the humongous kid bursting out from his clothes, they were in shock. "He will need to take this blood test as soon as possible . . . tomorrow?"

My mom saw the worry in Dr. Robinson's eyes and her answer was, "Yes, of course, doctor." She grabbed the laboratory papers and headed out the door.

As she came out, she told me about the blood examination I had to have the following day. I really could not have cared less, because I was starving. It was almost ten a.m., and I hadn't eaten anything. She told me to hold her purse and sit down. She approached the receptionist and made an appointment for the next day at eight a.m.

"Let's go," she told me. I knew something was wrong. Her eyes were sad and red, and her ever-present smile had disappeared. Her walk wasn't her usual strong walk; it was more of an ashamed amble. She was walking slow and without a purpose, with a slouched back and falling shoulders. We reached the car, got in and headed home, but the ride also felt slouchy and ashamed. It was a very quiet, rainy day. I didn't ask her what she had talked about with the doctor, and she decided not to tell me anything.

As planned, the next day I got up around six-thirty a.m., took a shower and got ready. I was going to take the blood test and, once again, I had to be fasting. I prepared a peanut butter-jelly sandwich for after the test; I wasn't planning on starving myself again.

We got to the hospital and it seemed abandoned—desolate. No other patients were there so early in the morning, just us. Only a couple of lights were on, in the waiting room and at the receptionist's desk. They had just opened, and I was going to be the first one to be tested. We went to the receptionist, turned in the lab papers the doctor had given my mom the day before, and sat down. About five minutes later, a nurse called my name. I stood up and left my sandwich on the seat. The nurse smiled and told me, "This won't take too long, and then you can eat your breakfast."

It was the quickest and easiest test ever, I thought. It had taken five minutes. How was a simple test going to change my fate? I came out and headed straight to my seat, unwrapped the protective napkin surrounding my sandwich, and started eating it, like a starving lion. Meanwhile, my mom approached the receptionist and asked when the results were going to be available. "Tomorrow," the receptionist said. "We'll send them to your son's doctor as soon as they're ready."

We walked out and my mom still had that sad gaze. Once again, the ride back home was long, quiet and rainy. Only the raindrops hitting the windshield and the music on the radio could be heard. As my mom drove quietly, I was thinking about my breakfast.

The sandwich was only the snack before breakfast.

The next morning, I held the phone next to my ear.

"Good morning, Alberto, this is Doctor Robinson. May I speak with your mom?"

After a long uninhabited, yet, dominating silence, I told him, "She's not here. She's working." I said this with a nasty tone.

He asked for her cell phone number and to get him off my back, I gave it to him.

As I was saying the last digit, my dad touched my shoulder and told me we had to go—he was dropping me off at school.

"Okay, I'll call her. Have a good day," the doctor said.

My response was a cold and definite "Bye."

It was only eight a.m., the day after my blood test, and he had called already. This was a bad start to the first day of my second semester of ninth grade.

My fourth-period class was starting when my teacher handed me a hall pass that said *Go to Office at 1:30 p.m.* Something wasn't right. The doctor's early-morning phone call, my mom's sad face, my family worries, and now, leaving school early? When the clock struck 1:30, I grabbed my backpack and headed for the door, telling my teacher I had to go. She dismissed me and, as I was walking toward the attendance office, I spotted a gray truck outside. "Is that my dad's car?" I asked out loud, like a crazy person talking to the wind. When you start talking to yourself, there is something very wrong!

As I was approaching the Attendance Office, I saw my father. I asked him what was going on and his response was, "Go check out, we need to go."

I did so. As I climbed into the car, I asked him if there was something wrong. Had someone died? He smiled and told me that my mom was going to meet us at the house. "We need to talk about you and the doctor."

That was the last sentence of our conversation. A rage came over me. I was getting tired of *that* doctor, and this time I was ready to fight! I felt a diet was coming my way and I wasn't going to let that happen.

Home was very desolate. My mom hadn't arrived yet, and all the lights were turned off. I headed to the refrigerator and started preparing my lunch. My dad, mockingly, told me to stop eating because I was fat. I let that slap in the face go by. I wasn't going to respond. What was the point?

While my sandwich was in the toaster, my mom arrived. "Hello . . . Gordito!" she said as she was opening the door. The ping from the toaster exposed the sandwich I was preparing.

"Hi, mommy, how are you? What's going on? What did that doctor say to you?" I asked her in a very annoyed and spiteful tone.

She told me to sit down and called my dad to the table. She pulled two papers out of her purse and told me, "This doesn't look good."

"What doesn't look good?"

My dad jumped into the conversation and said, "Your blood test . . ."

"And your weight," my mom added, interrupting my dad. "Look! This is your weight." She saw the big question mark on my face.

Before she could say anything, I stood up and went to the kitchen. I grabbed the sandwich I had just prepared and, with the same hatred I had for myself, I threw it in the garbage. I walked to my room and closed the door behind me.

The three numbers that I had decided not to look at on the scale were the three numbers printed on the paper my parents had showed me. That was my reality check, and I had to deal with it. But how?

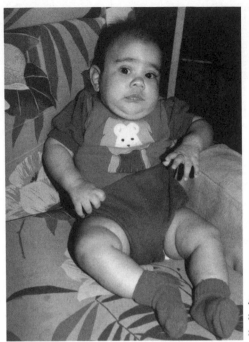

A baby Buddha with tamal and over-stuffed pita breads as appendages. December 1991.

First appearance as Curly: Short hair, big cheeks and tummy hugged by a shirt. 1996.

Tarzanian eighth birthday party. September 1999.

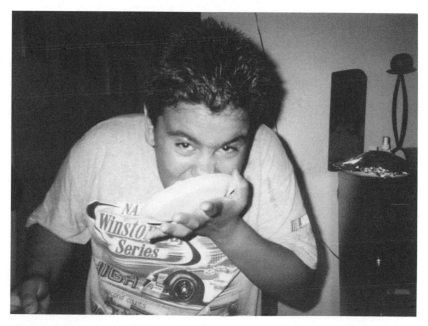

Do not touch my cake! My twelfth birthday party. September 2003.

My thirteenth birthday party with Mom and Dad (I'm wearing his shirt). September 2004.

The scene that broke the silence about my obesity—Me and my cousins, 2006.

Curly all dressed up. Looking good, no? February 2008.

Still working hard! Our worn-out faces say it all! Spring 2008.

New, improved me back in El Salvador. December 2008.

Mom and me. Smile! May 2009.

My best friend Megan and I. May 2009.

Healthy Bert—all the work
paid off! Summer 2011.

Chapter 11

Emergency Appointment
January 12, 2006

HOW MANY OF US HAVE MADE CHOICES THAT WE HAVE REGRETTED? All of us! I've made wrong choices; you have made wrong choices; all of us have made wrong choices! The famous philosopher Albert Camus once said, "Life is the sum of all your choices." Our choices give birth to consequences, and those consequences dictate the development of our lives. Sooner or later, those consequences come to life and teach us valuable lessons that should lead us to our personal fulfillment and help us reach the most important characteristic a human being desires and should have: self-love.

During my first thirteen years of life, I had made numerous choices about food, from where to eat to what groceries to buy. I also had decided to not visit a doctor. Now, those choices had produced an outcome, leading me to the climax of my young life. I was faced with the biggest choice ever. I was going to see what I had lost and what I needed to grow as a human being: self-love.

"What are you saying?" My grandmother screamed over the phone. My mom had her on speaker phone as she told her the results of my blood tests.

"He has diabetes? What? Do you know how terrible this disease is?!" she continued yelling.

I was sitting in between my parents, in front of the phone. I was silent. My breathing rate was increasing, my heart started pumping faster and my hands started sweating.

Did I know how perilous and cruel this ailment was? I don't know that I knew, until the day of my emergency appointment. But let me slow down the train and tell you what happened, step by step.

After my mom had shown me my three-digit weight, she dragged me to Dr. Robinson again. He wanted to discuss my condition face to face. It was an emergency! I was hesitant. I thought this talk was going to be like the lecture my parents received during our Salvadoran vacation, with everyone blaming them for bad parenting and pointing out my obesity and my flaws.

On the ride over to the hospital my mother said angrily, "You weigh. . ." her voice stopped and she took in a gulp of air, ". . . 230 pounds, and that is not normal for a fourteen-year-old who is five-feet-eight-inches tall!" She was slamming her hands onto the steering wheel as her timbre increased its intensity. She repeated this three times. That phrase stuck in my head the first time she said it. It stayed there for the entire twenty-minute ride, as if my mom had glued it with a hot glue gun onto my brain. I was at a point where I didn't have a comeback—I was speechless. Was I supposed to say "I'm sorry," or "It's not my fault" or "What do you want me to do about it?"

I, truthfully, didn't know how I had gotten to that point. I weighed almost as much as a newborn elephant. Most of my friends were my height or shorter, and they weighed between 140 and 150 pounds, which was normal. Nobody I knew weighed more than 200 pounds. I had never known someone who weighed that much, other than my dad, and he was about thirty years older than me and about eight inches taller. I was the same weight as my dad, although I was shorter, younger and dumber!

However, I didn't think my weight was unbearable or unhealthy, let alone deadly. Of course, I knew it was a lot of pounds, but what could it do to me? Beyond a doubt, I didn't comprehend the enormity of the crisis.

We got to the hospital and found Dr. Robinson was already at the reception desk, waiting for our arrival. Something was wrong! He seemed worried and in a hurry, as if something deadly was occurring. Was it me?

As soon as he saw us, he escorted us to an empty room. He was breathing hard and his right eye was twitching, just a tiny bit. His feet, one behind the other one, were going cuckoo.

The doctor rapidly settled and assembled himself and said, "Hi, we need to talk."

Without wasting time, he started explaining each part of my blood test results. He was going as fast as an exasperated bee, just giving us the amount of information our brains could digest. The first few minutes, we remained unruffled. Nothing seemed too wrong or out of place. He was going so fast that I really don't remember what he was telling us.

As he was turning to the last page of my blood test, he took a long breath and leaned toward us, and said, "Here's the problem. We need to talk about this one." His face was getting closer to ours as he continued. "This is the most important one. Normal blood-sugar levels, in a healthy person, range from seventy to 100 milligrams—fasting. Your tests were also fasting, right?" he hesitantly asked.

My mom and I nodded our heads up and down at the same time, but to reassure Dr. Robinson, my mom said "Yes, doctor, he hadn't eaten anything."

He showed us the paper. My three-digit result was far away from that 70 to 100 healthy reading. "This is your range," he said, "and your result is very close to the highest number. It's almost in . . . that range!" He ominously pointed at the red 124 milligrams. My blood sugar level was in the pre-diabetic range

(Above 125 means diabetes. And I was one milligram below that).

To reassure herself that those were my results, and in the hope of finding an error, my mom asked him, "Are you sure? Can you explain it, again?"

Once again, he went straight for the jugular, telling us that my blood-sugar levels were 124 milligrams. I was in the pre-diabetic zone. "Plus . . ." he added, standing up and helping me remove my shirt, "his neck, underarms and the area around his belly have a very dark pigment. This is called Acanthosis Nigricans; it is commonly a sign of pre-diabetes or diabetes. Also, he has low HDL cholesterol—the good cholesterol, and high triglycerides. This combination also goes along with pre-diabetes and diabetes. He also has high blood pressure. This mix of conditions puts him at a higher risk of a heart attack and stroke, which is worsened by diabetes."

I was shell-shocked and didn't know what to do or say. This talk took the wind out of my mom's sails. She started twitching and trembling. For a brief second, I thought I heard her stop breathing. After she stopped trembling, my mom started to cry and her mascara began running. She embraced her face with her hands and let it out. I could read her frustration and defeat in each drop that raced down her cheeks and splashed onto her pants. Each drop represented her love for me and her fear of letting me down, her fear of putting me in danger, her fear of letting me die.

As Dr. Robinson watched my mom collapse, he told me to wait outside, saying he needed to discuss some last-minute issues with her. I turned to my mom and my arms went around her. With my hug, I tried to tell her everything was going to be just fine. I looked right into her eyes and said, "I'll be outside." As I opened the door, I unconsciously turned back to my mom; her hands were yet again covering her face as the teardrops continued coming.

I was mute. I sat down on a brown couch and dropped my eyes to the floor. Each waiting minute became an eternity. What was Dr. Robinson telling my mom now? Were there more bad news?

I was so shaken up that, this time, not even my after-lunch snack was on my mind. Diabetes was the only word in my brain. I could hear Dr. Robinson repeating that word, on and on and on, nonstop.

As soon as my mom came out, she sat down next to me and looked me straight in the eyes. Her own eyes were destroyed from crying. She held my hand and told me that we needed to make a drastic change, a change that would benefit not only me, but them as well.

I didn't say "yes" or "no." I just didn't want to see her so miserable and disappointed because of me. My culpability was even bigger than my ego and my tire-like tummy. I didn't care if I had to go through another diet or visit a fat camp or completely stop eating. I just didn't want to see her cry, especially due to my irresponsibility.

I watched another teardrop roll down her cheek. This is enough! I thought. I was going to make a change, and I didn't care how big it was going to be. But I really didn't know what I was getting into. Mom started rummaging through her purse, looking for the paper that would bring me to the biggest decision I had ever made, and to the biggest outcome. I had to face a choice that was going to have a bearing on the rest of my life.

Chapter 12

A Done Piece of Meat

Same Day as Emergency Appointment

"PACKARD'S PEDIATRIC WEIGHT CONTROL PROGRAM AT LUCILE Packard Children's Hospital," said the paper. I grabbed it and told her I was going to think about it.

"Fair enough," she said.

Dr. Robinson's bad news bulletin had not only destroyed us emotionally, but it also had opened our eyes to what we had hidden. The news about my health brought my life into perspective. I stopped living for five seconds, stepped out of my body and saw what was going on. It was not pretty.

That same day, hours after the news, my mom decided to make a call back home to El Salvador. During the call, all hell broke loose, right through the phone. My grandmother learned that her first grandson might be the first to die. She disclosed her true feelings about diabetes and told my mother of her nonstop battle with it. She said she never wanted to see one of her grandsons suffer as much as she had.

My grandmother was diagnosed with diabetes when I was a toddler. She was a fifty-year-old lady who had to stop living her life freely due to this ailment. Because of this, she was petrified when she heard about my blood test results.

My grandmother had lost fifty percent of her eyesight, one of her kidneys has been slowly losing its function, and her pancreas wasn't functioning to its full potential. She needed to inject insulin daily, and because of it, her stomach was marked with small purple blotches. This ailment had been consuming her life, little by little. For her, every day was a new fight. Every day, it was a miracle for her to see daylight.

By the age of thirteen, I'd had an understanding of these facts. I knew how my grandmother's life had been affected by her illness. I had been around her through her ups and downs, but I never thought it could happen to me. I might have thought I was far away from it, but diabetes was right in front of me, nose to nose.

Once I heard my grandmother's voice begin cracking as she listened to the news about my medical condition, my heart stopped. The truth of my life slapped me in the face. In an instant, I was able to see my future diabetic life: injecting myself with insulin, losing my sight, having growth problems and then losing my life at an early age. I had been destroying my body, my temple.

I had only two options: give my life up to the devil, or make a change.

When I heard my grandmother begin to speak again, I unfroze. I fidgeted and goose bumps took over my body. I felt an enormous fear of dying, of throwing my life away.

It was time to stop it.

My mom was still listening to my grandma, and she had begun crying, too. Her head hung down as if she had lost the battle and shiny teardrops began to fall yet again. My dad couldn't take it; he had left the scene and relocated to his room. My grandmother kept talking, screaming and fuming. And there I was, sitting next to my mom in silence.

Then, right out of the blue, I softly and heatedly whispered "Stop!"

My mom turned to me as if she were telling me, "What the hell do you want to say? I think you've done enough!"

Meanwhile, my grandmother had asked in confusion, "What? Can you hear me?"

"I'm going into the program," I said quietly.

My mom looked worried and her eyes widened. "You don't even know what the program's about," she said. "You don't even know where it is! Plus, you need to be sure."

It's not that she didn't want me to try to change the outcome, but she didn't want me to make a decision I would later regret. Maybe she had dismissed the fact that, at that point, I was in a "live or die" situation. I didn't have a third option of "everything will be okay" or "don't worry." No! Either I give up on my life, or I fight for it. That is exactly what I was thinking. I didn't care what the program was or how it worked.

I told her with a determined voice that my decision had been made and I wanted to enroll in the program the next day!

I was fed up with losing this battle against Obesity. Dr. Robinson had told me I was literally footsteps away from diabetes. I had heard my grandmother tell me she didn't want me to suffer. I realized that Obesity was about to win the fight, and I wasn't going to let that happen. I was determined to stop it! I had found my voice and strength again. I knew that, if my family saw my desire to change, they would encourage and support my decision.

And my decision was irreversible.

Chapter 13

I Want that Glow

Following Day, January 13, 2006

FIRST THING THE NEXT MORNING, MY MOM CALLED AND SET UP an appointment with the program's director. I was so scared, I was about to poop in my pants. I felt as if Fat Camp was waiting for me, a camp in which they were going to rape me emotionally, try to make feel like crap for being obese and make me exercise like crazy until I vomited my guts out. Nevertheless, as I said before, I knew this was my last opportunity, and I was determined to make it work. "Hi, my name is Cindy Zedeck, and I'm the director of the Weight Control Program," she said as she welcomed us into her office.

Cindy seemed nice, approachable and skinny. She had an appealing glow I had never seen before on anyone. It was a godly, alluring glow that demonstrated her self-confidence, self-love, self-respect and self-pride (everything I was lacking). As soon as I defined the glow, I said to myself, I want to have it, too.

This time, I wasn't scared of her or anyone. There was something about her that made me trust her. Believe in her. Feel comfortable enough to put my life in her hands. I felt that she knew what she was doing: saving a life!

Once again I was weighed and measured. She showed us my BMI and the famous curves on the chart Dr. Robinson had shown us days before. That measuring and explaining took only ten minutes. The rest of the meeting was about the Weight Control Program, my new, imminent, healthy lifestyle and me!

"Tools, tools and more tools," Cindy said, right off the bat.

"No diets? You're going to make me eat what you tell me to eat, right?" I asked.

Cindy giggled and explained that the program was not there to impose diets or regimens. "Life is not about incarcerating our body," she explained, adding, "Of course, the program is hard and long . . . "

Believe me, the program was long. It consisted of my mom and me meeting with Cindy and the rest of the group—there were five other families that also had joined it—once a week, one hundred and eighty days. I know it sounds off-the-wall crazy, but once Cindy explained the following, the craziness became normal and the normal began appearing as the right thing. This is what Cindy exclaimed: "We cannot force your body and your mind to change from one day to another; we have to go slowly, so your body starts accommodating to the new changes, little by little. Otherwise, if we want to go right in and beat it up, we might do irreparable—moreover, dangerous, life-risking—damage."

Finally! The sunshine came upon me. Birds began singing and a picturesque rainbow invaded the horizon. The reason why diets don't work had finally been revealed to me!

You begin a diet in the hopes that your body will accommodate to the stress of this new, food-less lifestyle in a matter of minutes. You grow this image in your head that your stomach will, instantly, shrink. You'll lose forty pounds, you'll automatically become a toothpick, and life will be the way it was supposed to be.

It would have been crazy to go from a ball of fat to a tiny little thing, small as a toothpick, in a matter of days. Going from flab to "fab" instantaneously is unattainable. Additionally, if I wasn't meant to be a toothpick, then why would I push my body in that direction? Maybe I was merely supposed to be a grasshopper-like, or cucumber-like, or salamander-like person! But NOT a toothpick!

"We won't tell you to eat this or that, or not to eat this or that. We will give you easy tools to use so you can start building a healthy lifestyle," Cindy said. "These are some of the tools:

- Identify and avoid high-calorie, low-nutrient foods
- Develop better exercise habits
- Reduce sedentary behaviors
- Follow a healthy, balanced diet, even in difficult situations like family gatherings, holidays and parties
- Maintain a healthy weight over the long-term

Cindy said that, by using these tools, "Your reward will be a healthy life, which you *will* enjoy, not only for now, or tomorrow, but forever!"

This was the first time I had heard anything as coherent as her advice. Cindy told us she was going to be our "coach," which got me even more ecstatic. She was going to be the person introducing the tools and making our lives . . . how can I say this? . . . a bit less difficult. For the first time, I felt that there was someone out there hoping the best for me and something decent waiting for me. Someone and something with humane intentions were going to try to change my life instead of just trying to get paid. Here was someone who seemed to genuinely care for me, without even knowing me. Cindy became like my fairy godmother. She was going to be sitting on one of my shoulders, watching over me and my family. It was so refreshing to know that she believed I could live a happy life.

After the chitchat, laughing and introductions, she took two pieces of paper out from her drawer. "This is challenging, I know, since you're so young," she told me. "But your mom cannot make the decision. She can help you and persuade you, but she cannot make the decision for you. So, momma, you have to back off, just a bit, this time!"

Cindy handed a "contract" to me and said to take 10 minutes to think it over. The contract was just two pieces of white paper in which I was declaring I was entering the program willingly, without anybody forcing me to do so. In other words, the decision was in my hands. If I messed up, there was a chance my life would be a wreck. Or it could be the opposite scenario and I would live happily ever after.

Cindy told me she didn't want my mom to make my decision, since any result, good or bad, would become her responsibility and an excuse for me to blame her, instead of looking at myself first. She wanted me to examine myself and ask myself if I, in reality, wanted this. If I needed this. If I deserved this. She wanted me to realize why I considered it necessary to make such a mammoth adjustment in my life.

When my grandmother had been telling us about her life with diabetes, I had no doubts about entering the program. Point blank, nothing was going to change my verdict. However, once I heard about the length of it—including the words "grueling" and "challenging" in the same hour—plus the requirement of my unconditional 100-percent effort, I was horror-struck. I didn't want to bust my butt off only to find, at the end, that there would be no results—just like my attempts at dieting. I was scared of taking a chance and wasting my time and my family's time, again. Cindy stood up and told me that this was a moment in which I needed to reflect on my past and talk to myself about what I wanted. Alone time with myself. As soon as she left the room, I turned to my mom and broke the first rule.

"What do you think?" I asked her.

My mother giggled and said, "Don't look at me! Don't do it for me or for your dad or for our family. Do it for yourself. If you are doing it to make others happy, you are just going to make your life a living hell. And if so, let's just stand up, leave and forget about this."

I agreed. I wanted to be sure this decision was mine. I had made that mistake so many times, doing something not for me, but for the sake of others, just to fulfill some expectation they had of me. I always ended up hating it and them.

"Why do I want to enter this program?" I asked myself. "Because I don't want to become diabetic. I don't want to be injecting myself with insulin the rest of my life and have purple dots covering my belly. I don't want to die young. I don't want my pancreas to get ruined. I don't want to be perceived as a weirdo. I don't want to be isolated. I don't want to feel like I'm worthless, a waste of time, a waste of space or a piece of blubber. I want to not only make my parents proud, I want to make myself proud as well. I want to be able to trust myself. I want to be able to walk straight and with no shame. I just want to learn how to like and love myself. But this program is going to be really long and hard. I don't know what to do."

"Let's call Cindy back in," I told my mom.

Before she got up, she wanted to know what I had decided. I told her I was going to make my decision as soon as she left the room, and it was going to be a surprise.

My mom was hesitant. I saw the panic in her eyes. I knew she wanted to enter my little brain and know what I was thinking, but I wasn't giving away anything. She would have to wait.

"So, what did you decide?" Cindy asked when she returned.

I gave her the two white papers back, folded. I turned to my mom and noticed she had a crap-he-is-not-going-to-do-it look. I knew she was a bit disappointed, but the ironic part was that Cindy hadn't even unfolded the papers.

Cindy unfolded the contract. She didn't say anything, nor did she look up. She looked at the papers very carefully and quietly. Then she opened her drawer, put the contract in it and took a "Welcome to the Weight Control Program" pamphlet out.

I was going to do it. The best reward I got that day was seeing my mom's smile come back. Minutes after receiving the "Welcome" pamphlet, I grabbed the phone and called my dad to announce my decision. His answer was a simple, music-to-my-ears, "I knew you were smart."

I felt so pleased with myself, as if I were doing myself a favor. It was as if my body had been waiting for that moment for so long, and finally I had made it happen. I was happy—and nervous, of course, but mostly happy.

"Be ready. Our first meeting is Monday at three-thirty," Cindy told me as she gave me a hug.

Once again, I felt reassured that they really cared about me, not just about getting their paycheck.

From that day on, my parents became my sidekicks. Cindy became my fairy godmother.

Chapter 14

Greens, Yellows & Reds

First Meeting, January 16, 2006

Our lives improve only when we take chances—and the first and most difficult risk we can take is to be honest with ourselves.

—Walter Truett Anderson

THE FIRST MEETING WAS UPON US. THE WEEKEND HAD FLOWN BY as fast as the wind and I had been so worried, my head full of nonstop thinking about how the rest of the families were going to welcome us, what the first challenge would be and about the first tool we would learn. Of course, I thought about the first pounds I was going to lose. All of that caused a mix of emotions and restlessness.

The night before the meeting, my grandmother, Uncle Atto and Aunt Lorena called to wish me luck and to let me know that the distance between us was a minimal obstacle for the support they were pouring out toward me. I liked that feeling of encouragement, that extra push. The love!

That night, after talking to my relatives, I laid out my clothes, a notebook and a pen. I kept reminding my parents about the exact time we had to be at our first meeting: "Remember, tomorrow at three-thirty. So, Mom, what time are we going to get in the car? Do you think we're gonna make it on time? We know how you're always 'fashionably late.' Should we leave an hour earlier? Remember, I need to be there at three-thirty, not three thirty-one, like you usually do!"

My parents were so irritated with me, they nearly exploded: "What the . . . what is wrong with you? You're so wacky. Wacko!" my mom laughed. Then she added with excitement, "You have to be well-rested for tomorrow, so go to sleep. Maybe I should tie you to the bed." I know she would have, too. And my dad would have helped her.

Finally, it was Monday afternoon. My mom picked me up from school around three o'clock and headed to the building where we were going to meet. The twenty-minute ride was nothing compared to our ride back from the hospital, the day the blood test results came back. This time, I filled the car with my nonstop talking. Every thirty seconds, I would ask my mom a different question about what she was hoping for the program.

Exactly ten minutes before the set time, we were parking. At that same moment that the breaks were pressed, my stomach churned and my right eye twitched This time, I wasn't backing down; there was no way!

I embraced my mom's hand, with my trembling, panicking one, and wished her "good luck." Her response was a kind-hearted and jubilant smile! We walked side by side until we reached the classroom where we were going to meet. As I entered, I recognized Cindy, who approached and welcomed us. Next to her there was another skinny, glowing lady.

"Hi, my name is Thea, and I will be working with you guys, too," she said.

I felt fortunate; I knew I was in the right place and time and was putting my life in the right hands.

The space was vibrant and multi-hued—not very big and not very small, but welcoming and warm enough for my taste. It was as if I had entered a healthy land. Exercise posters and pictures of vegetables and fruits hung from the walls, including happy broccolis, robust carrots, apples and bananas jumping up and down. The green carpet gave us the feeling of being at a park. The room contained seven white tables, with two comfortable white chairs at each one; there was also a white board at the front, which had a big, red "Welcome" written on it.

It was perfect. The other families seemed very excited, too, and happy to meet us. It felt as if we were been introduced to our temporary, new family . . . and that felt wonderful! I was fitting right in and my mom was happy to see that I was happy, and that I felt like I was part of something.

The clock announced three-thirty and Cindy officially welcomed us. As she was talking, Thea began to pass out separate binders for the teens and their parents. Each binder had the description of the weekly tool. The binder was going to be our agenda and memory; if we didn't remember the lesson of the week, we could easily find it in there. In other words, it took away our ability to make up excuses.

The first lesson was entitled "Pay attention: write and classify them." "You'll be writing down what you eat," Cindy explained.

The first tool was simple. We were asked to pay attention to what we put in our mouths, write the name of the food down, and classify it.

Next, Cindy gave us another piece of paper with drawings of veggies and fruits on the borders, and a title that said "Reds, Yellows and Greens." As this paper landed right in front of our faces, Cindy held a copy above our heads and told us to write down what we had eaten so far that day. She pointed at the paper with one index finger.

Here is how the first attempt at journaling what I had eaten looked like:

- Breakfast:
    - Eggs
    - Beans
    - Juice

- Lunch:
  - Hamburger
  - French fries
  - Soda
- Snack:
  - 6 cookies
  - Soda
  - 3 chocolates

Nothing seemed out of place! Perfect breakfast, right-on-point lunch and an exquisite snack! As all of us were finishing up, Thea began passing out small, spiral notebooks that said "Green, Yellow and Red Light Foods."

"What are they talking about? Green? Yellow? Red? Are we playing traffic lights?" I wrote on a piece of paper in my unintelligible cursive. I slid the note to my mom, and she turned her head and seemed annoyed as she told me to "Pay attention." I turned back to Cindy, who was explaining that "This little booklet has all the foods you can imagine. They are classified in three colors: Green, Yellow and Red."

As she continued talking, I couldn't contain my confusion, so I started flipping through the pages until I reached the explanation of the colors.

The first entry was "Red Light Foods," which are very high in calories and contain amounts of five, or more, grams of fat. They tend to be awfully heavy on the grams of sugar—ten and up—and they have little or no nutritional value. We were instructed to stop and think before eating red light foods, since they can be very fattening and unsatisfying. One of the goals for the program was to eat fewer than ten Red Light Foods per week!

There was also a warning at the bottom of the page: "Sweet-tasting foods like cookies and cake are habitually Red Light Foods, since the sweet taste usually means the food has a lot of sugar, which means extra calories your body doesn't need.

Moreover, foods that are swimming in butter/oil or have been cooked with large amounts of fat are considered Red Light Foods, including french fries, chips, ice cream and fried chicken. Also remember that some foods are converted into Red Light Foods due to what you cook them in and with what you cook them with!" And more: "Don't fry . . . bake! Don't fry . . . broil! Don't fry . . . grill! Don't fry . . . boil! Don't fry . . . sauté! Don't fry . . . eat healthy! And if oil is required, use less than two tablespoons per dish."

Phew! That was a marathon!

The next page explained Yellow Light Foods, which are the ones that have a small amount fat—five grams or less—and of sugar—less than ten grams—but also are filled with needed vitamins and minerals. These include some very nutritious and required foods, such as grains, pasta, poultry, meat, fruits, bread, cereal and most vegetables. These foods are acceptable to eat at any time—but in moderation.

As I was reading the last section, I heard the classroom growing quieter and quieter. Seconds later, I felt a shoe tapping on mine. It was my mom's warning. I immediately elevated my gaze and the first thing I noticed was Cindy's dagger eyes on me. My face was red with embarrassment. I had been caught—during my first class!

"Alberto, you have to *pay attention*," Cindy said. "Why don't you read out loud what Green Light Foods are?"

I turned to the section titled Green Light Foods and read, "Green Lights Foods are foods with less than two grams of fat and poor in sugar, yet, they contain multiple vitamins and minerals needed by our bodies. You can eat almost as much of these as you want. These are very nutritious, for example: tomatoes, cucumbers, carrots and the most famous and hydrating, water."

After we had learned what each color meant, Cindy gave us our first assignment: "Classify what you have eaten today. Write the color you think each food was."

I turned to the page where I had previously recorded what I had eaten that day, and I wrote the following:

- Breakfast:
    - 2 Eggs—2 yellow
    - Beans—yellow
    - Juice—yellow
- Lunch:
    - Hamburger—yellow
    - French Fries—yellow
    - Soda—yellow
- Snack:
    - 6 cookies—yellow (??)
    - Soda—yellow
    - 3 Chocolates—yellow (??)

As I finished writing the last "yellow," Cindy asked me if I'd like to volunteer and go up to the board and write my results. There was no way of getting out of this one. My mom even pushed me to get up. I had to. So I got up, grabbed the black marker and wrote down the foods. Then, with the red marker, I wrote how I had classified them.

"Eggs are yellow, correct! But did your mom fry them with oil?" Thea asked.

I didn't know, so my head, slowly, turned to my mom.

She said, "Yes, with oil."

Thea looked at me, raised her eyebrow, and said. "So then, your eggs are a Red. Remember, when you cook a food with a Red Light Food like oil, that food automatically becomes Red."

I erased the "Yellow" next to eggs and wrote "Red."

For the rest of the foods on my list, I didn't even have to ask. I knew my beans had been refried in oil, meaning they became a Red.

"What about my orange juice?" I asked.

Thea answered with a question. "Was it 100-percent orange juice?"

Once again, I turned to my mom, looking for her to save me, and repeated the question.

My mom immediately responded, "Yes! I used oranges to make it and no sugar was added, since they were incredibly sweet and ripe—they were quite perfect for orange juice!"

Thea looked at me, with a hopeful grin and said, "Correct!"

Finally, I had gotten one right! That was a boost to my self-esteem and seemed to stop my uncontrollable sweating.

Once I got to the "Lunch" part of my food diary, I saw that my enlightened moment was going to darken up with more Red Light Foods.

Cindy asked me, "Did your hamburger have mayonnaise and American cheese?"

This time, I couldn't turn to my mom. I had eaten lunch at school; therefore, it was all on me. By the way, I had the opportunity to lie. I could have taken that moment to introduce my tricky mind. But if I had done so, I would have been lying to myself—not anyone else.

"Both," I answered.

"Okay, that indicates there were two Red Light Foods. Thus, write next to hamburger two Reds."

French fries? I didn't even have to ask her, and I didn't want to experience another ignorant moment. I knew they were a Red. I don't think I have to explain why. The name says it all. French *fries!* I automatically changed the label on the fries, categorizing it as a Red, and quickly moved on to my soda. A regular soda with more than a dozen grams of sugar? Realistically, it wasn't water, much less 100% natural! In other words, it was synthetic and full of uncontrollable sugar! It equaled to a Red; no doubt about it!

My desperate, sweating disappointment grew when my pupils look at the word "Snack." I had discovered, in the Red

Light Food description, that cookies and chocolates were definitely a Red, since they are full of lard and a multitude of sugar. I had written "Yellow" next to both my snacks, thinking Cindy and Thea would miss them. I thought I could make them go unnoticed. Fake them. I was trying to hide reality, once again.

Thea instantaneously jumped to her feet and announced, "No, Alberto, you know what they are!"

I'm such an ass! I had been defeated and put on the spot.

I decided to erase everything and re-write it. The final product turned out to be as the following:

- Breakfast:
  - 2 Eggs—2 red
  - Beans—1 red
  - Juice—1 yellow (the only correct one!)
- Lunch:
  - Hamburger—2 red (mayo + cheese = 2)
  - French fries—1 red (duh!)
  - Soda—1 red
- Snack:
  - 6 cookies—6 red (scary!)
  - Soda—1 red (another one!)
  - 3 chocolates—3 red

Total: 17 Red, 1 Yellow and 0 Green.

Seventeen Red lights in a matter of five hours? Yikes!

I was surprised as I read the board. It was so scary to see that most of my diet was made up of Red Light Foods. This felt like a very big slap in the face.

I had gotten the idea of how to use the first tool they had given us. I knew where they were coming from and the reason I needed to pay attention. They were trying to open my eyes and teach me the reality of what I was eating. They didn't want me to waste my time by writing everything out; they wanted me to be aware of what I was eating.

The first exercise had put everything in perspective and taught me where I had to make changes. My first task was to watch what I put in my mouth.

Writing and classifying had taken almost the entire class. As we were wrapping everything up, Cindy said, "Inside your binder, you will find more papers like the one we used today to write what you have eaten. Use them and write, every day, for the entire program what you eat! Classify your foods. Try for fewer Red Lights each week, and I want to see more yellows and greens!"

The first meeting was over and it had been a total success. The first tool seemed uncomplicated. I felt I had everything under control. I knew what I had to do and why I was doing it. I grabbed my binder and said good-bye to everyone. As we all were heading toward the door, Thea called out, "Be honest when writing; don't lie to yourself!"

Cough, Alberto, cough! Nice, Thea! Way to put me on the spot, again!

The happiness, fire and motivation I'd had the night before were still in me; my self-love was growing bit by bit every minute, and my motivation was stronger than ever. My happiness at that moment was extraordinary. For the first time, I was feeling ready to fight the fight . . . and dance.

On that night's ride home, I turned the radio's volume to maximum and started to dance to "Boogie Night." I told my mom, "This is cool. I like it!"

She turned and vividly smiled as she agreed. "Keep in mind it's not going to be flowers, sunshine and rainbows all the time. But you, me and your dad—we will succeed, okay?"

Keep it coming, Mom! I loved it! I was so ready for the next meeting. I wanted it to be the following Monday already!

As soon as the golden doorknob turned and my dad's face appeared on the other side of the door with a "How did it go?" my mom ran to the kitchen, her high heels clattering along the floor. She opened every single drawer and door in the counter, as if it was a war against time, and began classifying and throwing things away. She got rid of all the Red Light Foods! Then she classified the others, with my dad as a sidekick helping her out.

Was my first health persecution over? Not yet! Was classifying foods over? Not yet! Was there more work? Certainly. Was it going to be hard? Believe it!

Green Light Foods

Vegetables

- Artichoke
- Arugula
- Asparagus
- Beans
- Bean sprouts
- Beets
- Bok Choy
- Broccoli
- Brussels sprouts
- Cabbage
- Cauliflower
- Carrots
- Celery
- Cilantro
- Corn
- Cucumbers
- Eggplant
- Fennel
- Jicama
- Leek
- Lentils
- Lemongrass
- Lettuce
- Mushroom
- Cactus
- Okra
- Onions
- Parsley
- Peas
- Peppers
- Potatoes
- Radishes
- Rutabaga
- Scallion
- Sweet potatoes
- Snow peas
- Spinach
- Squash
- Taro
- Yam
- Water chestnut
- Watercress

Beverages and Condiments

- Broths
- Club soda
- Horseradish
- Lemon Juice
- Mustard
- Vinegar (any type)
- Perrier Water
- Soy Sauce
- Water

Herbs and Spices (all you can think of)

- Allspice
- Basil
- Cayenne pepper
- Chives
- Cinnamon
- Dill
- Dried mustard
- Dried fennel
- Ginger
- Herbs Provence
- Paprika
- Rosemary
- Sage
- Thyme

Yellow Light Foods

Bread

- Bagel, Plain
- Bagel Chips
- Biscuit
- Bread: white, wheat, whole wheat, etc.
- Bread crumbs
- Bun: hot dog or hamburger
- Croutons (no fat)
- English Muffins
- Pancake, plain
- Pita bread
- Rice cake (unflavored or flavored)
- Roll (small diameter)
- Tortilla shell
- Soft Tortilla: corn or flour
- Waffle, plain

Crackers and Snacks

- Cheese tid-bits
- Chex Mix
- Goldfish
- Graham
- Nuts, all; a handful no more than three times a week since high in fat
- Pretzels
- Rice cakes, all
- Ritz, plain or cheese
- Rye Krisp
- Saltines
- Soda
- Vegetable thins

Juices

- Apples
- Grapefruit
- Orange
- Pineapple
- Tomato
- Juices sweetened with Splenda/NutraSweet
- Pear
- Pineapple
- Plums
- Pomegranate
- Watermelon
- Jellies and jams, sugar-free or sweetened with Splenda/NutraSweet, etc. Ex. *Smuckers*
- Syrup, 100% pure maple syrup or 100% honey

Fruits (all you can think of)

- Apple
- Applesauce
- Apricots
- Banana
- Blueberries
- Blackberries
- Cantaloupe
- Cherries
- Grapes
- Grapefruit
- Kiwi
- Lemon
- Mango
- Nectarine
- Orange
- Papaya
- Peach

Dairy (milk, cheese, etc)

- 1%, skim or fat-free milk
- All reduced fat cheeses
- Cottage cheese, 1%, fat-free
- Ricotta cheese, 1%, Fat-free
- Frozen yogurt, fat-free
- Cream cheese, fat-free
- Yogurt, fat-free; Ex. *Dannon*

Fast Foods

Chinese Take-Out Foods

- Beef with broccoli
- Chicken Chow Mein
- Chow Mein noodles
- General Tso's soup
- Hot and Sour soup
- Hunan tofu
- Kung Pao chicken
- Moo Shu pork
- Soup noodles
- Stir-fried vegetables

Japanese Food

- Ebi (shrimp), boiled
- Gohan (rice)
- Kaibashira (scallops)
- Maguro (fresh tuna)
- Miso soup
- Misoshiru (bean paste soup)
- Natto
- Saba yakisakana
- Shioyaki ("Swimming Trout")
- Soba noodles
- Somen noodles
- Steamed crab
- Sunomono
- Surimi
- Tako (octopus), raw

KFC (Kentucky Fried Chicken)

- Colonel's rotisserie gold chicken (without skin)
- Corn-on-the-cob
- Garden rice
- Green beans/Mean greens
- Mashed potatoes and gravy
- Red beans and rice
- Skin-free crispy side breast
- Vegetable medley salad

McDonald's

- Chicken fajita
- English muffin
- McGrill chicken classic
- Salads:
    Chef salad
    Chicken oriental salad
    Garden salad
    Fajita chicken salad
    Shrimp salad
    Chunky chicken salad
- Salad Dressings:
    Lite Vinaigrette
    Oriental
- Breakfast Foods:
    Cheerios
    Egg McMuffin
    (with no bacon)
    Wheaties

Red Light Foods

Candies

- Caramel
- Chocolate
- Cough drop
- Fudge
- Snickers
- Jelly beans
- Life savers
- Lollipop
- Mints (cream)
- Gumdrops
- Hard candy
- Marshmallows
- Peanut brittle

Cookies/Crackers

- Small or large, Ex. Pepperidge Farm Chocolate Chip, Oreo, etc.
- Animal crackers
- Brownie
- Ginger snaps
- Vanilla wafers
- Teddy graham

Cream

- Cream cheese, regular
- Half and half
- Heavy whipped or unwhipped
- Non-dairy whipped cream
- Light table
- Non-dairy creamer
- Sour cream, regular, light, non-fat
- Tofutti

Cheeses

- Blue cheese
- Brie cheese
- Cottage cheese (with 2% milk or whole milk)
- Cheese spread
- Ricotta cheese (with 2% or whole milk)

Milk-Beverages

- Cocoa/hot chocolate
- Diet hot chocolate
- Eggnog
- Instant breakfast
- Milkshake
- Whole or 2% milk
- Milk: chocolate (whole, 2%, 1%)

Milk Desserts

- Pudding (made with whole milk)
- Pudding (made with skim milk)
- Yogurt:
  Flavored
  Frozen, regular

Fats and Oils

- Butter
- Butter Buds
- Butter Salt
- Margarine
- Margarine (diet)
- Oil (all of them; except a small amount of olive oil per day)

Jellies and Jams

- Apple butter
- Flan (2%, 1%, fat-free milk)
- Jam, jelly, marmalade, regular
- Jam, jelly, marmalade, diet
- Jello, regular, diet

Pies

- Custard, 1 crust 9"
- Fruits, 2 crust 9"; ex. apple pie
- Lemon meringue
- Pumpkin pie 9"

Frozen Confections

- Ice cream (Breyer's/Sealtest/Perry's/ Ben & Jerry's/Haagen Dazs, Baskin Robbins)
- Ice cream, chocolate-covered bar
- Ice cream, soft
- Ice cream soda
- Ice cream sundae
- Ice cream cone (plain without ice cream)
- Ice milk
- Italian Lemon ice
- Fudgesicle
- Frozen yogurt bar
- Gelatin pop
- Kool pop
- Popsicle
- Pudding pop
- Sherbet
- Sorbet

Beverages

- Fruit drinks and punches: Hi-C/Hawaiin Punch/Orangeade
- Gatorade
- Kool-Aid
- Snapple
- Soda (except "diet" sodas)
- Quinine water
- Tang
- Tea, iced, canned (with added sugar only)
- Tonic water
- All alcoholic beverages (only for 21 and older)

Cakes

- Angelfood
- Cake, plain
- Cake, with icing
- Cheesecake, regular; you can find a Yellow Version in Chapter 20
- Cream puff
- Cupcake (with or without icing); you can find a Yellow Version in Chapter 20
- Éclair
- Fruit cake
- Gingerbread
- "Hostess" Cakes: Ho Ho's/Twinkies, etc.
- Strawberry shortcake with or without whipped cream

Chapter 15

My Head in the Toilet Bowl
February 2006

Have the courage to say no. Have the courage to face the truth. Do the right thing because it is right. These are the magic keys to living your life with integrity.
—*W. Clement Stone*

"REPEAT 'NO!' THREE TIMES," CINDY DEMANDED WITH A FIRM tone of voice, as soon as we walked into the next meeting. We hadn't even warmed up our seats or gotten a glimpse of the big red NO on the board when she made that demand.

As I was trying to imagine the reason behind it, I said to my mom, "Last week, we learned how to classify foods. This week, we learn how to say no?"

She turned to me and replied, "It's crazier than home, huh?"

We all, as a group, said "No!" three times.

"Great! Now you have the next tool," Cindy told us.

"Wait! What?" my inner voice said out loud.

"Yes! This is your tool: saying 'No' when needed. Is there a problem, Alberto?" Thea asked.

My neck became stiff and my face felt like plastic. I couldn't nod or smile or blink or move my lips; no response was forthcoming. I didn't want to make a fool out of myself by asking what the tool was, because maybe the rest of the group understood it. Instead, I raised my gaze and said "Sorry."

Cindy started her explanation: "Saying no can be hard, right, Alberto?" she asked—a silent nod from me. "I know it wasn't understandable at first, but this ability is very important. It will dictate how you act in difficult situations when you encounter Red Light Foods at birthday parties, family reunions or simply when you go out for lunch with friends.

I was catching on; everything began making sense, and the question mark was erased from my face. My confused mind relaxed. It was as if the clouds parted and I was seeing the light.

"When to say no is the big question," Cindy continued. "Possibly when you know you've eaten a large amount of Red Light Foods and you don't want more. Or maybe you really do not want those extra Red Lights. Or maybe you are satisfied and do not want anything else. Or maybe you want a Yellow Light Food instead. Or you simply don't want anything else to eat."

"There can be a very simple reason behind why you don't want another Red," Cindy said. "But here's the problem. Sometimes we don't want to say no to Red Light Foods because we don't want to hurt the feelings of the person that is offering them. Or maybe you are dying to eat that Red Light Food, or maybe peer pressure leads you into eating it, or maybe you don't want to feel as if you're on a diet, right?"

That was my problem. I knew when I didn't want a Red Light Food or when I was getting to the "satisfied" point, but saying no wasn't part of my nature.

Her coherent discourse led me to decipher the reason why I had thrown up my guts two weeks earlier, at a family reunion.

A Required Digression: Our family reunions are memorable for the love and great fun we have together. They are the times that are engraved in our minds and impact our lives. But when you're offered three turkey sandwiches and you don't know how to say no, you might end up half-naked, on your knees, with your head inside the toilet bowl.

I was finishing my third week of the program when Aunt Dinora's celebratory luncheon popped up. I had been apprehensive about attending because I knew how much food would be available all over the house, and I was still trying to get the hang of classifying my foods—especially the reds.

I was still adjusting to the program trying to resist my cravings for Red Light Foods. Certainly, when you're fourteen and live with your parents, your voice doesn't count very much in regards to attending family gatherings. You do as they say. So there was no way to skip that party.

My inner self was telling me during the entire drive to my aunt's house—five red lights and three stops and five miles of driving—to avoid them! "Whatever you do, don't go near them! Just run away from them! Do not talk, look, smile or glimpse at the bad foods!"

As we arrived, the first words coming out of my aunt's mouth were, "Welcome! Have some chips," and she placed a bowl filled with chips on my hand.

It was like a cold bucket of water had been thrown in my face. I caught a glimpse of the chips, and a big red light turned on. I knew chips were forbidden, since they are fried in tons of oils, and I was trying to get away from them. But of course, once you have a plate filled with chips, almost glued to your hand with a hot glue-gun, it is very hard to say no or give them back. I had to swallow what my inner voice had told me on the way there. So I grabbed the bowl and sat on the sofa, where all my cousins were already sitting watching television—not much had changed since my twelfth birthday celebration.

After waiting for fifteen grueling minutes, one of my cousins announced that lunch was served. The turkey sandwiches they had prepared were plated. With the bowl of chips I had already eaten, I didn't know if I was ready to continue chewing and swallowing. But the magical word wasn't going to come out of my mouth.

Lunch was served, which meant eating was demanded. As I was walking toward the kitchen to grab my plate, I was already seeing multiple plates with two sandwiches on them. There was nothing wrong with the sandwiches. Sure, maybe they should have let others choose the number of sandwiches they wanted, but over all, everything seemed smooth. The sandwiches appeared very healthy and Yellow. I was able to see the skin-less piece of turkey lying on a bed of lettuce topped with tomatoes and radishes. They didn't seem dangerous or very Red.

But, as I got closer and closer, I saw my aunt putting a very thick layer of a white, cream-like substance on the inside of each slice of bread. There was the problem: a thick layer of mayonnaise. Another Red Light Food. "Get away!" my inner voice screamed.

I wanted to run away from the sandwiches and hide. It felt as if every step of the way, the sandwiches were right in front, behind me and next to me. They were taunting me and trying to break me, as if I were the laboratory rat and they wanted to know at what point I was going to break down. I didn't know what to do. But again, the plate holding the two mayonnaise-daubed turkey sandwiches was glued to my hands.

"For my dad?" I asked my aunt, praying to God, Buddha, Allah and every entity you can imagine, for her response to be "Yes."

She turned around and gave out a very loud, cackling laugh and said, "No, silly, for you!"

What I most feared had just happened. These sandwiches weren't returnable. I was trapped. I didn't know where to turn or what to do. I wanted to say "No!" but I couldn't, since I felt that accepting and eating two turkey sandwiches was mandato-ry, a request that needed to be accomplished if I wanted to be part of the family. Also, I didn't want to hurt my aunt's feelings. I predicted she would feel I wasn't appreciating the hard work she had put into the luncheon if I blew her off. Thus, as a respectable, young, voiceless teen, I grabbed my plate and headed back to the living room where, once again, I glued my butt to the sofa—just like my cousins.

Eating two sandwiches was over-indulging.

Just then, a silver platter with all the leftover sandwiches appeared right in front of me. The platter parked itself right in front of me, without saying "excuse me," between my eyes and the television. It was there and it was impossible to avoid seeing it.

My gaze raised to see my aunt smiling as she held the platter. She grabbed a sandwich, practically put it on the tip of my nose and began showing it off. She asked, "You want another one?"

My brain was saying no. My conscience was saying no. My stomach and pancreas were saying no. In fact, my entire body was saying no and was disgusted about even the smallest possibility of tasting another piece of turkey.

But of course, as all of my body parts were saying no, my heart was melting as my eyes gazed into the warm eyes of my aunt. Those puppy eyes and that little-girl smirk were taking over my entire body. How could I turn her down?

"*Another* one?" my mom, perplexed and flabbergasted, asked me, emphasizing the "another."

My sight rapidly ignored her line of fire and turned to the television as my mouth took the first bite of the third sandwich. I knew I was doing something wrong, but I felt I had to. After eating the third sandwich, my stomach started growling and making a bubbling noise. I was burping the turkey back out. Every burp had a different taste: turkey, onion, radish, chips, a mix of it all; it was revolting. Suddenly, an acidic taste crossed my tongue, and a burning sensation entered my throat. Once I felt that, I knew what was coming: a flood of small, undigested pieces of food, a lunch medley. I got up and ran into the bathroom to fill the toilet bowl with the undigested lunch.

Everything came out.

Why couldn't I just say, "No, thank you, I'm full" or "I'll eat it later" or "I'm just gonna eat one and a half" or "Can I just have half of the third one, without mayonnaise?" or "Instead of another sandwich, can I have a piece of fruit?"

I know it would have been hard for me to say those words, various versions of "No." But what would you rather go through the hurtful moment when you say "No," or vomiting your life out?

I told Cindy about this situation. She giggled and then explained it to me in a way that put the situation in a new light: It's okay for you to feel remorseful. You didn't want to hurt anyone's feelings. I shouldn't tell you this, but to build a new lifestyle and learn how to take care of yourself, you might have to be a little bit selfish. You have to think about yourself. Maybe this sounds a bit shallow, but when you get sick, or you get diabetes, or you vomit, everybody else's lives will continue. But for at least that moment or for the rest of your life, yours will stop!"

At the time, it did sound unfeeling, selfish, and over the top—but isn't it true?

From that day on, I said to myself, I will never let anyone or anything push me to a point in which I end up puking everything out!

Chapter 16

The Donuts Did Me In

April 2006

Mistakes are a part of being human. Appreciate your mistakes for what they are: precious life lessons that can only be learned the hard way.

—Al Franken

WHY WERE MY PARENTS ALWAYS RIGHT? I TRIED TO LOOK AT THE situation through rose-colored glasses, to make it less overwhelming, and they tried to be realistic. I tried to believe everything was going be easy-breezy, but they broke the charm. They didn't mind my optimism, but they didn't want me to underestimate the power of the tools. Sadly, the injudicious part of me didn't listen to them, and I would fall back again.

The first three months were all about learning how to catalog foods and feel comfortable, letting my body settle into the new, healthy way of living without pushing or starving. I was trying to get the hang of it, trying to make good food choices a part of my second nature, but most of all, I had to learn to pay attention. Those first few months were also about losing the first few pounds.

I had lost more than twelve pounds since I started the program! I was losing about three to four pounds per month. At first, that total seemed like nothing. I felt like I was working hard, but my progress was insignificant. Thea and Cindy saw my frustration, and I know they were worried I would quit. One day, they sat me down on a brown leathery sofa and parked themselves in front of me, as if I was in the principal's office.

"Your weight loss is going to be slow, but it will be a great achievement. The body can't lose thirty pounds in a month. That would be injurious to your body, to have to adjust to all these changes in so little time. Your body would go crazy, and you would feel as if you were starving yourself!"

Cindy gave me two thumbs up and concluded, "You're on the right track, and you'll lose much more!"

This meeting recharged the vanishing fire in me. That boost was what I desired and needed in order to persist. Everything was going smoothly until Spring break came around.

Previous Spring breaks, for me, had meant staying at home every day, watching television and eating. I kept everything I needed in one place so I wouldn't have to move much. This Spring break fell within the six-month program, so I thought it was going to be different: hale and hearty. But I got caught in the obesity trap.

From eight in the morning until four-thirty in the afternoon, it was me, me and me, alone in the apartment without the righteous eyes of adults. My parents were at work. I was responsible for my actions, nobody else. I was the one who had to tell myself, "Don't eat that, eat this instead" or "Watch out for Red Light Foods" or "Pay attention!" But when you have a supermarket right in front of your face, 24/7, and you have the opportunity to buy whatever you're in the mood for, the phrase "Don't eat that, eat this instead" becomes a bit more challenging.

On Monday, when watching television grew boring, I went to the kitchen. *What do we have?* I asked myself as I opened every single cabinet door and the refrigerator. I saw crackers, pretzels, orange juice, strawberries, bananas, boiled beans, 100% wheat bread, blueberries, carrots, fat-free cottage cheese, popcorn kernels and much more. These foods were there waiting for me as if they were on a silver platter with "Yellow and Green Foods" signs everywhere! Unfortunately, nothing seemed appetizing.

I found myself craving something decadent and sweet. Without giving it much thought, I put my shoes on, grabbed my keys and closed the door behind me. As I was walking toward the supermarket, I already had an idea of what I wanted. *Only a piece. It's going to be good,* I told myself. I tried to make believe what I had decided was reasonable. I was making myself believe it was right, even though I knew it fell on the wrong side of the fence.

The automatic doors opened and a sweet aroma of recently baked donuts traveled to my nostrils, sending an I-want-them signal to my brain. I walked toward the bakery department and saw a poster announcing, "Donuts, Fresh and Delicious from the Oven."

Fresh? Did that mean organic and healthy? Delicious? Did that mean I could have them all? Oven? Did that mean they weren't fried? Thus, no Red Light? I walked back and forth in front of the donut counter, thinking. In the back of mind a voice was shouting, "Stop! Don't do it. Look, there are rice cakes and you have so much fruit at your house. You can even make a fruit smoothie!"

Many red flags were raised in my mind, but I went ahead and grabbed a white bag and paid the one dollar and fifty cents for the donuts. My mouth was watering and I was just hoping to get to my cave so I could eat in private. Minutes later, I was opening the front door of my house, racing toward the sofa and switching the television on.

I took a donut out of the bag, and the aroma overwhelmed my entire body. The glazed donut was shining like a goddess coming to save me. Five minutes later, the shining goddesses were gone—gone before my show had even started. *It was good and nobody saw me. What they won't know won't hurt them.* The next day, the same scenario unfolded. As I was sitting on the couch, the word "fresh" crossed my mind along with the memory of the recently baked donuts' aroma in my nostrils.

I left the house and walked across the street as fast as I could. In a matters of minutes, the automatic doors opened. Again, I headed to the bakery counter, but this time, I ordered a bag of twelve donut holes. The "fresh" sign was still up there, so I could tell myself that eating them was an okay thing to do; *they're baked and fresh!* Once again, I went back home, sat on the couch, watched television and devoured the donuts while I waited for my parents to come home from work.

I had gone from "only one time, only one piece" to "only two times, only two pieces" in less than twenty-four hours. I was falling back into the dark hole I had spent months trying to get out of. Every day that week was exactly the same. I was going to the supermarket and buying what I wanted and pretending it wasn't bad at all. I was making myself believe that the donuts were Yellow Light Foods, since I didn't know how they were made—plus, they were "fresh" and "baked." Wasn't I acting like a know-it-all? Trying to act smart? Making up stories, knowing they were wrong? I was pretending I knew what I was doing and believing it was true and correct. I was lying to myself And instead of going forward, I was falling backwards.

When I went to our next meeting, I felt as if a cold bucket of water was thrown at me. During my routine weekly weigh-in, I saw the white numbers begin to change as I stood on the scale. I was very confident I would show that I had lost an extra pound or two, and that I was still on the right track. The donuts and donut holes had disappeared from my mind. It was as if those incidents had never happened: they were like dreams! I didn't even remember them—until the numbers on the scale stopped.

"You gained three pounds," Cindy said, her voice full of disappointment. My mom looked at me with eyes wide-open. She was so shaken up that she just started mumbling. The irony of it all was that, as soon as the numbers stopped, I knew the cause.

"We have been eating right. We've used the tools. Nothing bad," my mom told Cindy. "I mean, he's been on vacation from school, but he continued with the program . . ." My mom turned to me and angrily asked me what had happened.

My eyes dropped to the ground, remorsefully, as my inner voice was mocking me. "I've been eating donuts," I whispered to my mom and Cindy.

They both still looked confused. I think they understood that I had eaten donuts, but they wanted to know how many, since three pounds aren't gained by eating a single donut.

I stood there quietly for a minute before opening my mouth again. I needed to choose between feeling deceitful or guilty. Should I come clean and move forward or pretend it had happened only once? I had missed the chance to act shocked about where those three pounds had come from; however, I would have violated a golden rule: "Be honest with yourself." Finally, I blabbered as if there were no tomorrow. I told them what had happened. I told them about the "fresh" and the "baked" on the poster. I told them about making myself believe that one piece would not alter my life. I told them I had acted like a bighead, thinking I had everything under control—and now, of course, the weight said it all. In simple words, I had been foolish and irresponsible.

My mom was dismissed from the weighing room. Cindy said she wanted to talk to me by myself, without influence from anyone else, including my mom's hostile eyes. She just wanted me and her, face-to-face and nose-to-nose.

She sat down and began her speech: "I understand that you miss those types of foods, but just for now you should avoid them. I am not saying that you will never ever eat them again, but for now, try to avoid them."

Then she continued with an analogy that made me understand further: "You're like a drug addict. You're addicted to bad, non-nutritious, tasty food. Because of that, you need to stay away from those foods until you're ready to control yourself around them."

I lowered my head in shame. I knew she was right. I hadn't been able to control it. I couldn't even go to the supermarket by myself without picking up Red Light Foods the minute I walked in. I wasn't able to make conscious and correct, food-wise choices—yet!

After listening to her for almost ten minutes, I opened my big mouth and asked, "You say I will eat those foods again—but when?"

She looked into my eyes, giggled a little bit, and said that she didn't want to make me feel as if I was in a "food jail" where I was going to eat only what they said. Then she said she was going to answer my question with a single word: rewards.

"We're not playing a game or taking a test that will earn me a reward. So what do rewards have to do with me losing weight?" I asked her.

Cindy answered, "First and foremost, this is not about losing weight. Remember? This is not a diet. It's about building healthy eating habits. Everyone can lose weight by using diets or starving themselves, but those ways do not teach healthy habits. You would probably regain whatever you lost. Second of all, rewards are given when you do something good or have accomplished something; otherwise how would you do something good? Set goals for yourself and accomplish them. Tell yourself, 'I will only eat ten Red Light Foods this week' and if you succeed, maybe you can get a reward such as a serving of orange sorbet, which is the best food from the worst list. Ask for one with less sugar or fewer grams of fat, but DO NOT ask for a double chocolate chip piece of cake with fudge on it. In other words, choose the reward that will make you feel good and maybe even give you a tiny amount of nutrients, not the one that would make you feel lazy and sluggish. Remember, if you eat too much sugar, you'll end up crashing. Then you'll probably end up sitting in front of the television or taking a nap." That wasn't all. Cindy continued, "Also, remember: a reward is not given on a daily basis, but rather, from time to time, just like a present. You don't get a daily present; you just get one when you deserve it or when the right time comes, such as on your birthday. A reward shouldn't be five donuts or half a chocolate cake or one entire bucket of chocolate ice cream with fudge on top, just like a present cannot be an entire clothing store. For example, if my reward is going to be ONE Red Light Food, then I have to be conscious of the serving size. A serving should not be bigger than your hand. So if, as a reward, I would ask for a piece of cake—but when I cut the piece of cake, it equals two servings the size of my head—then you're taking advantage of the situation and being unreasonable.

"Choosing the best food from the Red Light Foods is called the 'differential of foods.'"

This was the first time I heard of "differential of foods," although I didn't comprehend it completely, I understood that I should make decisions between the "best from the worst" and the "worst from the worst." In this way, I would choose what was beneficial and worthwhile. In other words, if the "best from the worst" is better and satisfied me the same way as the "worst from the worst" would, then I should choose the "best from the worst," since I wouldn't sacrifice my satisfaction. But if the "worst from the worst" is still the winner, then go for a small portion of it and enjoy every bit of it.

Cindy reiterated that losing weight and looking thin and handsome and hot are only secondary results. The most important outcome of using the new tools is building a new healthy lifestyle. A secondary effect is that that lifestyle will end up with me shedding some weight.

Chapter 17

Is It Going Away Forever?
Late April 2006

TELEVISION WAS A MESMERIZING BOX THAT HAD ANCHORED MY head and eyes. Every time I came home from school at three p.m., the first thing I did was turn the television on. There was no thinking, no breathing; flipping on the switch was a systematic part of my routine. I'd open the door, put my bag next to the television, reach for the remote control and go into my magical (fantasy) world. Being apart from it, after we had been so close, was a pain. I would sit and eat in front of it; I would do my homework without missing a piece of the show. Some kids go to bed reading or listening to bedtime stories, but I would go to sleep listening to and watching television. In the morning, I would wake up to my favorite shows.

Television had been deteriorating my social skills, little by little, but at the same time, I felt it was the only one who didn't judge me. Television accepted me the way I was and gave me the chance to explore new worlds, in a matter of minutes, without moving. I treated television as if it were a real friend of mine, as if it were a person who would talk to me whenever I felt alone, a person that I could rely on whenever I needed it.

It was the fourth month since I had joined the program. Spring was nearly over and the first hints of summer were surfacing, which meant the program was reaching its end. At first, it was scary to know that, in less than eight weeks, Cindy and

Thea would let us spread our wings and fly. I worried as I counted the number of weeks left.

But as soon as they told me what the next challenge was going to be, my eyes not only opened, they nearly burst out of my face. Out of the open blue sky they dropped the challenge. I was livid, even though my mom was just smirking next to me, enjoying every bit of it. Mom knew it was going to be the hardest challenge yet, and I was going to complain to no end, but she also knew there was no way to back down from this tool.

"This is your new challenge," Cindy said, after she had told us the name of the tool: Television Turn-Off.

I was screaming in my seething mind as they were explaining the challenge for the second time. Every time they would say "no television," my stomach churned.

The bad news led to another face-to-face talk with Cindy and Thea. I'm pretty sure they saw my ravaged face. That's probably why they called my mom and me into a private meeting room and sat us down.

"We saw you were a bit disappointed," Thea said to me.

As calmly as possible, I explained that I couldn't stop watching television, first of all, because "all my new shows" were coming up, and second, because "I like it."

Cindy looked straight into my eyes and said, "We know!"

They knew I was addicted to television, the same way I was addicted to Red Light Foods. I had lost control over it, and if I didn't create boundaries between me and it, I was never going to be able to be the controller; instead, I was going to be the controlled one. I needed to show that I was the boss, but I didn't know if I wanted to be the boss.

"How many hours of television do you watch?" Thea asked me.

My mom jumped into the conversation and said, "He watches about five to six hours a day and on the weekends, he watches more than seven hours, sometimes eight."

I glared at my mother.

"More than forty hours a week?" Cindy asked, flabbergasted. Then she said, "Look, we need to change that. Will you try this challenge? If you accomplish it, you'll have a great tool for the rest of your life. If you don't watch television, you're going to have more time to do whatever you like to do. For example, maybe you like reading or walking."

Thea added her piece: "And you'll decrease the amount of food you eat. Because when you're in front of the television, you forget what you're putting in your mouth, since you're hypnotized by what's on the screen. You forget the amount you're eating. You forget what you're eating. Your hands just grab and travel to your mouth without you knowing what you're putting into it, just like a robot.

"Also, thousands of food commercials are shown on television; once you see a juicy hamburger or a chocolate cake on the magic screen, you start desiring it. We know you don't want to torture yourself or go back to your old habits. So if you decrease the amount of television you watch, you'll see fewer food commercials, and you'll decrease the amount of Red Light Foods you eat. Besides examining what you are eating, this is an opportunity for you to grow as a person and to find out who you are and what defines you—or at least find out what you like."

They were good saleswomen, but I wasn't too sure I wanted to buy it. I know for a fact that they got the message that I wasn't very interested in this new tool, so they stopped wasting their words and ended the talk. We returned to the meeting room, where the rest of the group was waiting for us.

My mom and I sat down, and Cindy and Thea walked to the front of the room where, for the third time, explained the challenge. They repeated everything they had told me in the private meeting and added even more. I knew they were trying to convince me to try the new tool, but I wasn't sure I wanted to.

"What do you like to do, other than watching television?" Thea asked everyone.

My mind was blank. There was nothing! Why did I have to think so long about what I liked to do? Television had consumed me to the point where I had forgotten who I was, what I liked, what I did for fun, and what defined me.

Thea was now asking each person what they liked to do. When she got to me, my mom kicked me under the table and asked me, "Don't you like painting and drawing . . . oh yeah, and swimming?"

I turned to her and a light bulb went on. My mom had come to my rescue. I had taken art classes before and I had loved swimming since I was five years old. But television had separated me from them. "What she said!" I told Thea with a bit of excitement in my voice.

With the exhilaration of my brain and heart as they recalled all the genuine and authentic fun I'd had painting and swimming, it was like I had woken up from a trance. One clear-cut question snapped me back from my memories.

"And why don't you do these things anymore?" Cindy followed Thea's question.

I didn't want to answer the question, even though I knew the right answer; in fact, everybody knew! I couldn't say it.

"Is it because of television?" Cindy asked. "Your TV-watching time doesn't let you participate in those activities?"

I wanted to close my ears. I didn't want her to be correct, but unfortunately—or I should say, fortunately—she was. She had said the answer I didn't want to say or think about, and her remark had facilitated my decision-making about whether to try the new tool.

After opening the door of doubts about television, Cindy said to all of us: "That is the point of this challenge. We don't want to deprive you of television. We just want you guys to do something other than watching television, because there is a real, breathing world outside of that magical box."

They were giving us the opportunity, by taking television out of our houses, to go to the park or paint or swim or play or dance or cook or clean or hang out with friends or do whatever we always wanted to do. They were opening a new land of possibilities. Cindy handed us a paper in which she described the new tool. It said: "This week is all about replacing television with different and fun activities. Choose the three you like the most. Try to participate in them instead of watching TV. Choose activities YOU like and enjoy and savour your time doing them. This tool will teach you how to gain control of television."

I was scared. My legs were shaking, my pits were sweating, my cheeks were red and my guts were churning. Something inside of me was telling me this new tool was not going to work. I knew I was obsessed with television, even though I also knew how malicious it was. I knew replacing it was going to be hard, but I had to give it a shot.

This week is going to be hell, I told myself as Cindy and Thea were wishing us luck. I knew I was going to need more than luck . . . more of a kick in the butt and a helping hand as well.

The Unraveling Week

I was only three steps away from the remote control, but I couldn't use it. The magical black box was right in front of me, but I couldn't turn it on. It was talking to me, "Gordito, turn me on! I have your favorite shows!" It was tempting me. It was heartbreaking to know that something so good was so bad—and so close.

To make the story short, this is what happened and how I handled it.

Monday

After the meeting where we heard about the Television Turn-Off tool my mom and I entered our house. My obsessed, animal instinct told me to put my bag next to the television and grab the remote control. But my mom quickly jumped over me, snatched the remote control away and said, "I'll take that." She put it in her pants pocket.

About a minute after our arrival home, boredom kicked in. Once again, my instinct told me to go turn the television on. I was so fixated on watching TV that I quietly went into my room, pretended I was going to change clothes, closed the door and turned my television on. I lowered the volume and sat on the edge of my bed, leaning forward, close to the TV's speaker. I knew I was putting myself at risk of getting caught, but my fixation was so strong that I didn't care.

Just as I was getting comfortable, my mom entered, walked over to me very calmly, grabbed the remote control and turned off the TV. Then she sat next to me and said, in a whisper, "Go do your homework. Don't be a masochist!"

"But what if I like being . . .?"

She interrupted me. "This is a tool, and we will at least try it. I know you may not like it . . ."

Then I interrupted her by howling, "MY SHOW IS ON! Why can't you just give me a minute? GOSH!"

Had it worked? Was the manipulating gene still in my DNA? She leaned over, put the TV on and threw the control into my hands. It had worked!

When sixty minutes had gone by, she came into my room and once again turned the TV off and took the remote away from me. "ENOUGH!" she shouted. "Go do something! TRY! Do you understand what that word means? TRY! Don't just sit here as if you don't have anything to do! DO SOMETHING!"

My fun was over, and her temper was steamy. So, due to the fact that I love my life and didn't want my mom to strangle me, I had to find something to do. This is I what I did:

- I finished my homework. For the first time, it was error-less.
- Later on, my mom asked me to set the table and to help her plate the vegetables, which I did. I don't remember ever, *ever* helping my mom set the table.
- During dinner, instead of watching television, for the first time I was able to savor my dinner without distractions, to taste every ingredient, enjoy every bite and pay attention to how much and what I was putting in my mouth. Moreover, *we talked to each other!* First time ever! Something new to me. We were able to communicate and share our thoughts! My dad even said, "You are very talkative tonight!"
- After dinner, my parents and I went on a walk and kept talking!
- Once we came back from the walk, I prepared my backpack and outfit for the next day as we continued talking!
- Finally, sleep time!
  The first day was over. For the first try, I think it went okay.

Tuesday

I didn't miss TV during school time—well, maybe a little. The hardest part was during my alone time. I had promised myself to try my hardest not watch it. I didn't want to sit on the couch and be tempted and tortured by television, so that Tuesday I avoided it by:

- First, I put a yellow towel over the TV-set with a sign that read, "DO NOT TURN IT ON. IF YOU DO, YOU SUCK AT LIFE!" I had found a way to make myself think before turning the television on, and it also gave me a small laugh!
- Mom and I walked to and enrolled in the nearest gym. I jumped into the pool (still, with my T-shirt on). I felt like a

fish being thrown into the water for the first time in years! I felt joyful . . . I felt like myself.

- When I returned home from the gym, I started my home-work and once again finished it without a mistake. After-wards, I helped my mom in the kitchen and helped serve dinner.

- When dinner arrived, we sat down and once again savored, smelled and appreciated our food and its spices. One factor I loved and was overindulging in was the talking part. We talked . . . again . . . to each other! I was able to talk to them about school. Wow! Amazing!

- Following our second memorable, loquacious dinner, we went for a stroll around the neighborhood, and we kept chatting like a normal family! My normal family.

- The same as Monday, after our walk, I prepared myself for the next school day.

The Multi-million Dollar Question: Did I watch television? I did! Yet again, I couldn't go the entire day without watching some. I couldn't detach from it so quickly; it was too hard. Step by step! But that night, I watched it for only forty minutes, right before going to sleep, instead of watching it for more than an hour.

Wednesday

By the third day, being TV-free had become a bit more man-ageable. I still missed the magical box, of course, but I was get-ting a grip on how to control it. Instead of whimpering around like a sad dog begging for television and food, I decided to play with it. That day, I discovered something in me: I'm a low-key, healthy chef! I cooked Hot Bert Faux Fries as a side dish; sim-ple, but with a delicious crunch! (Recipes can be found in the end of the book.) Believe me, cooking and using my time in a productive way felt much better than sitting down without any-thing to do, like a lump!

Wednesday was a successful day. I was able to do something I had learned to like and could control. And of course, the food was amazingly tasty.

The Multi-million Dollar Question: Did I watch television? I did, but this time I had reduced it to thirty minutes. Was I fol-lowing the rules? Maybe yes, maybe no, but I felt proud of try-ing and giving it my all. I was going slowly, but I was reaching success!

Thursday

The same as Wednesday; I decided to continue playing with food. This time I did my Spin-a-berry Salad and Healthy Bert's Chili.

My self-pride and productivity levels were increasing steadi-ly, the same as my gaining control over television. My need to watch it was decreasing and fading away.

The Multi-million Dollar Question: Did I watch television? You know the drill . . . I did. But I had reduced it to twenty min-utes. Only twenty minutes before going to bed; not an extra minute. My Twenty Minutes Rule was born.

Some might be thinking that I was lying to myself or evad-ing the challenge. But I wasn't. I was trying my hardest to con-quer an addiction.

Friday

By Friday, everything was a walk through the park. I was still tempted to have the black box speak to me. I had to shut up the voice in me telling me to watch it. I couldn't believe I was handling it so well. In just a few days, I had built a new habit and had destroyed an old one that had taken years to con-struct. Instead of being a couch potato, I was becoming a good cook, a competent swimmer and a help around the house. But most of all, my family and I were becoming a "real" family.

Saturday

I had awakened indisposed that day. At first, I believed Saturday was going to be the hardest day without television. We usually stayed at home all day and sat in front of the TV, watching it from nine a.m. to five p.m. I was panicking, inside and outside.

But weirdly, it turned out better than I had expected.

Thanks to the "Television Turn-Off" tool, Saturday became the Home Cleaning Day.

- I cleaned my room, which was a jungle of clothes and shoes and multiple smells.
- I used the vacuum and dusted the living room. Plus, my parents and I did laundry, and my mom taught me how to clean the bathroom.
- Then, after cleaning and a well-deserved shower, my mom and I began cooking. This time, we cooked Chicken Bertlets. After lunch, my parents and I went for a walk around the neighborhood and ended up at the supermarket, we rated the entire supermarket from top to bottom, from Red to Yellow to Green.

Later that night, I helped my mom with dinner. Once again, sitting down at the table, all of us together and communicating, was magical. Talking to my parents was a new habit for me. After dinner and cleaning the table, the handy Twenty Minutes Rule came in.

Sunday

Out of the entire week, Sunday was the hardest day without my black box. We stayed home the whole day, except when we went to noon Mass. After church, we came back home and started making lunch, which was grilled chicken with Orzo salad. Once lunch was over, my parents decided to take a nap while I stayed in the living room with nothing to do. I could have drawn, but I wasn't in the drawing mood. I could have gone swimming, but the gym was closed. I could have gone for a walk, but I didn't want to go by myself. Once again, the television started calling my name at the moment when I was the most vulnerable, the moment when I needed someone to talk to. Finally, around four p.m., my parents woke up and, together, we went on a stroll around the neighborhood. I made it the longest stroll we'd taken, turning on every single street I could find until we got lost. My mom got mad, and we decided to come back.

When we were back home, I got my books and clothes ready for the next school day and with my mom started thinking about what we could cook for dinner. We finally ended up making simple ham and mozzarella cheese sandwiches—easy and tasty, especially when you add a pinch of rosemary and use Dijon mustard!

The dinner once again was new for me. I couldn't get used to it, but I liked it. And then, of course, the Twenty Minutes Rule arrived, followed by sleep time.

Voila!

The week was over! The week I had dreaded was finally done! I'd learned about myself and learned a new habit: controlling myself. I had outgrown television, and my life wasn't revolving around it anymore. Television became a lifeless object. It was no longer my life. But what were Cindy and Thea going think about my Twenty Minutes Rule?

"How was your week?" Cindy asked us as she was going around the room. This time, I didn't wait to be put on the spot. I raised my hand above my head and went right to the heart of my decision on the Twenty Minutes Rule.

Surprisingly, Cindy reacted as follows: "That's Okay. Good J-O-B!"

It was a great relief, and I was able to breathe and open my eyes bravely, even though I hadn't accomplished the challenge. I knew I had given it my all and I felt proud of myself. I knew Cindy, Thea, my parents and everyone else felt proud of me, too!

Right after I began breathing again, Cindy told us that the Television Turn-Off wasn't to deprive us of watching TV, but to gain control over the television habit. As soon as she said "control," I proudly smirked. I knew I had gained power over television. With my rule, I was able to control the amount of television I watched. I didn't let television tell me what I should do. Without television, I had been able to create new dishes and rediscover my love for painting and swimming. Most of all, I'd found the ability and time to enjoy and reconnect with my parents, especially during dinners. We were a normal family again!

Chapter 18

I Laughed, I Cried and I Lost
Mid June 2006

Nothing splendid has ever been achieved except by those who dared believe that something inside them was superior to circumstance. —Bruce Barton

THE PROGRAM HAD REACHED ITS EXPIRATION DATE. CINDY AND Thea were about to let us spread our wings and fly. They had taught us everything we needed to live a healthy life, and now it all depended on us if we wanted to use those skills.

Our last meeting wasn't just liberating us from the Monday meetings;, it was a time to reflect. It was time to consider my self-destructive past, the lack of self-love I had experienced; the hard work and persistence I had put in during the past six months; the challenges and tools that helped me reconstruct myself, from the inside out, and most importantly, the pride I felt in accomplishing the program and re-creating myself. The Lucile Packard Weight Control Program had saved me from becoming a diabetic and had handed me tools to help regenerate and rebuild my life from scratch.

My weight loss was a "secondary effect" of my healthy lifestyle. This secondary effect had led me to the self-fulfillment and self-pride for pushing and trying as hard as I could for six months I discovered the most important ability of a human being: the ability to love yourself.

Tools I Came to Love

SELF-HONESTY: Stop lying to yourself. Once you lie, there is no going back. You fall into that vice. Self-honesty is the first step to self-loving and self-respect.

PAY ATTENTION: Pay attention to what you put in your mouth. You will know what is healthy and what is not! Know your food! Classifying foods will give you the capability to control the amount of a specific food you eat, to decrease certain foods, to have more variation in your diet and to have a well-balanced life.

REDs, YELLOWs & GREENs: These are tools that will never leave you. Once you know which foods are red, yellow, and green, you will know which ones might give you energy, nutrients or a small case of sweet-hangover. Knowing these colors will help you to Pay Attention and have control over food.

SAY NO TO RED LIGHTS: Remember, if you fall, your life stops—but everybody else's life will continue. It won't hurt to say "No, thank you" or "Maybe later" once in a while. Try to say what you think.

THE BEST FROM THE WORST: This is the best way to go. You want to reward yourself for using the Tools and losing a pound? Or you just want to eat a decadent piece of food? Then reward yourself with the Best from the Worst. But remember, do not try to act smart by lying about the portion (don't eat anything bigger than your head) or about the type food you choose for yourself.

TELEVISION TURN-OFF: TV is the magical black box that doesn't let you go! Choose any type of activity and practice it instead of watching television. If you decrease your television time by thirty minutes per week and find a new hobby, it will be a win/win for you and . . . you!

ME TIME: Your body is your temple; don't let it deteriorate. Exercise! Choose any sport or physical activity you like. It has to be an activity you will enjoy, but it doesn't have to involve breaking your head against the pavement or destroying your sweat glands. It can be as easy as practicing a pastime you've forgotten about. The overall goal of Me Time is dedicating a small amount of time to yourself every day. Don't you deserve it? Love yourself!

Chapter 19

Lost and Found
Mid June 2006

THE BEST WAY TO END A POSITIVE EXPERIENCE IS WITH A BANG! I asked my mom to make an appointment with Dr. Robinson, the person who had introduced us to the program. This surprise request came from the same mouth that had decided not to visit doctors and the same person who had given up on medicine: I wanted to visit my doctor and check up on my health. They hadn't told me that visiting a doctor means self-loving, but it's common sense. Exactly three days after the farewell meeting, my first appointment in six months had arrived. For the first time since revolutionizing my eating and exercising habits and my overall life, I was going to step onto one of the entities I shrank from the most. I thought it was time. In simple words, I wanted to know how much weight I had lost.

I remembered the feeling I had had the first day I attended the program: the stomach turning, the pits and hands sweating? They came back! Although I had asked for the appointment, I was still a little bit hesitant to attend it. But now, to know the amount I had lost, I had to step onto a scale again. For a split second, I began doubting my hard work. It was one of those moments in which you ask yourself: Did I do the best I could? Could I have done a bit more? Will it pay off? I was fearful the results weren't going to be what I and everybody else expected. I didn't want to be a failure. Fear and panic invaded my mind.

As my parents and I went through the revolving doors of the hospital, I knew the moment had come. It was time to unveil the outcome.

I entered the same waiting area where, six months earlier, my mom had handed me information about the program, as I was sweating so uncontrollably that you might have thought I had run through sprinklers. After a few minutes of waiting, I was called by a nurse into the examination room. I was a nervous mess and about to run the other way. But thankfully, something unbelievable happened. As I was following the nurse, Dr. Robinson caught a glimpse of me. He walked over to where I was, tapped me on the shoulder, and said "Alberto! You look amazing! I'll be right there."

I was speechless. I couldn't even say, "Thank you." I was so relieved. That compliment stopped my sweating and worrying. I knew I had done something right. I knew from his reaction that my hard work had paid off.

The moment of truth had arrived. Dr. Robinson came into the examination room and led me onto the scale. A bit of the sweating came back as I climbed onto it and planted my feet. I tried to exude confidence. I felt as if I had reached the top of Mount Everest. I stood on the scale with my head held high and my back rigid. The numbers started changing. One hundred. One hundred and sixty. One hundred and eighty. Have I lost any weight? The increasing numbers were very reminiscent of my earlier weigh-ins, before the program. The scene seemed similar. But the outcome was different this time. As the numbers reached one hundred and ninety pounds, they started slowing down. What the hell is going on? Is the machine broken? I said to myself.

"You can step off the scale. Let's go in here," Dr. Robinson said, indicating the examination room. I sat in one of the chairs, and my foot began tapping the chair leg. What had been the weight? I wasn't able to catch a glimpse of it. Dr. Robinson had pressed the Erase button before my eyesight lowered.

In the same way he had dropped the bad news during my emergency appointment six months earlier, he now dropped the good news. The three digits he was about to announce were the remedy to my anxiety. "Congrats! You've lost . . ." Dr. Robinson said as I interrupted him by saying, "Oh my God! Are you serious?" while I was looking at the three digits he had written down. But I couldn't celebrate by myself yet.

I stood up, fast-walked out of the exam room and went to the waiting area. I waved at my mom and dad and escorted them back to the examination room. I wanted them to rejoice with me. The same way they'd had to endure the bad news, six months earlier, I wanted to share the good news with them.

"I was congratulating Alberto. He has done an amazing job! Look, this is his new weight!" Dr. Robinson said to my parents as he was pointing at the new, three-digit number. I had lost 30 pounds! I had dropped from 230 to 200 pounds in six months!

My heart was jumping up and down. My parents' faces lit up as soon as they saw the numbers. My dad's hand went around me and squeezed the life out of me while my mom's lips traveled to my cheek and kissed me. To top it all off, Dr. Robinson said an extra "Congratulations!" as he was extending his hand to meet with mine.

I was graduating, with a diploma in my hand and great satisfaction in my heart. Moreover, I felt the most appreciation I have ever felt for anyone toward Cindy, Thea and Dr. Robinson. My Three Musketeers.

I had lost weight and the fear of the scale. That same day, I understood I could beat the scale if I aspire, desire and work at it. I had lost my anxiety. I had found serenity. I did finish those six months with a bang, don't you think?

But was my battle over?

I had shed thirty pounds, but I was still a work in progress. I was not obese, but I was still overweight. Obesity had managed to put more than sixty extra pounds on me. I had lost thirty of them, but if I did the math correctly, I still had many more to hammer down. The program, the tools, Cindy and Thea had opened the door to a better life for me. Now it was my turn to walk through that door and deliver. I knew how to do it, and I was going to do it! And I did do it! It's no secret!

Chapter 20

Getting Personal with my Inner Chef
Recipes

FOR THE PAST FEW YEARS, THE WAY MY PARENTS AND I PERCEIVE, catalogue and control food have changed, and so has the way we cook it. Since the Television Turn-Off, cooking is something I must do. I cook because I love it so much! It has become my hobby and a part of my daily routine, just like television-watching used to be. I have found that cooking is another way to control what I put in my mouth.

When you go to restaurants or supermarkets and you buy already-cooked food, you're not sure how it was cooked. They may have used week-old oil, or maybe they covered the food in margarine and/or mayonnaise. You really don't know what they're doing back in their kitchen, so when you eat that food, you don't really know what you will put in your mouth. Restaurants also choose what you will eat. You have to eat what's on the menu. Either you eat their food or you don't eat at all. They make the choice for you. In the kitchen of your home, it's the other way around. You have control over what you will cook, how you'll cook it, what Yellow Light Foods to use, and, what Green Light Foods to use. Plus, you get to cook what you're in the mood for. If you don't want pasta and instead you want a delicious beef patty, then you can have the patty. If you don't want chicken but you feel like pasta, then you have the pasta.

In your kitchen, you also have control over how to cook food. Maybe you don't want your chicken barbecued today.

Instead, you want it crispy and baked. In that case, you can cook my Chicken Bert-lets. It all depends on you.

If you have read the previous chapters, you know what the result was. In my past life, because I didn't like cooking, I would end up eating Big Macs, curly fries and fudge sundaes, nearly every day. Cooking is easy if you make it easy. You don't have to be the greatest cook in the whole wide world. If you can put together a healthy sandwich, that's good enough. But if you go in the kitchen with an I-don't-want-to-be-here attitude, then your chef-time is going to be the most miserable time of your day.

Once you're in the kitchen, you can make magic. You can make whatever you want, literally. You don't have to worry about cooking something too fancy. Use your imagination and use what you have. Do it the way I do! Every time I go in there, a new plate is created or upgraded. One day, I wanted some chicken and ended up making Bert Spicey Patties. Another day, I went in wanting some dessert and ended up cooking some Bert BB Bread and dipping it in fat-free milk! I mean, every time I go in there, it's like I'm an artist painting or sculpting a new creation. It's hard but delicious work.

Of course, I'm not going to talk about all my experiences in the kitchen, such as how I've created catastrophes. I'll share with you the delicious dishes; the ones in this book are only the amazing ones.

These are my own, personally tailored recipes. These recipes should act as healthy templates that you can use to create new, personalized dishes of your own. Your dishes can end up being better than mine! Moreover, these recipes are all Yellow Light Foods. This is a Red-free zone! This means you can cook every single recipe and not feel guilty or drowsy or slouchy afterwards. Instead, they will make you feel empowered, energetic, healthy and ready to tackle the world.

These recipes range from breakfast to brunch to lunch to snacks to drinks to dinner to desserts. I've modified many of my favorite dishes into the Yellow zone, such as mac & cheese, chicken cutlets, banana bread, strawberry cupcakes and even the most renowned American dessert: cheesecake. Renewing each recipe is all about having imagination, thinking about how you can lower the amount of fat or sugar or how you can replace or even omit the fat or sugar from a dish without risking the taste, texture or—most of all—your satisfaction.

Breakfast

Oatmeal A La Bert

Makes one serving.

Ingredients
- 1 cup of fat-free milk
- ½ cup of old-fashioned oats
- ½ teaspoon of cinnamon
- 1 pinch of salt
- 1 teaspoon vanilla extract
- ½ cup of dried berries such as blueberries, or you can use fresh berries (your choice)
- 1 tbsp. of Splenda or 1 tbsp. raw sugar or 1 tbsp. 100% honey

Procedures
1. Bring the fat-free milk to a boil. Add the oats; simmer until moisture is absorbed and smooth consistency is reached. Before turning the stove off, add cinnamon, salt and vanilla extract. Let oatmeal cool down.
2. Cut the berries in half (if you use strawberries, cut them in quarters) and mix them with the oatmeal. Add the sweetener of your choice
3. Enjoy this energizing breakfast!

Bowl of Life

Makes one serving.

Ingredients

- 1 cup of fat-free milk
- ½ cup of whole-grain brown rice
- 1 teaspoon of cinnamon
- ½ cup of berries (your choice), cut in half
- 1 teaspoon vanilla extract
- 1 tbsp. of Splenda or raw sugar or 100% honey

Procedure

1. Bring milk to a boil. Add brown rice. Simmer until rice is fully cooked. Let cool.
2. Cut and add berries; I like to use blueberry or blackberries. Add the vanilla extract and sweetener. Mix well.
3. Enjoy!

French Toast

Makes 2 servings.

Ingredients

- 4 slices of whole grain bread
- 4 egg whites
- 1 teaspoon vanilla extract
- 1 teaspoon 100% honey

Topping

- ½ cup frozen fruit
- 1 ½ teaspoon of 100% honey

Procedure

1. In a shallow pan big enough to hold four slices of bread, combine the egg whites, extract and sweetener. Beat lightly. Put the four slices of bread into the pan, and then flip them over to coat both sides. Set aside.
2. Heat a nonstick skillet or griddle over medium heat. Spray with cooking spray.
3. Remove bread from the pan, mopping up any leftover egg whites with the bread. Cook the slices in the pan for about 2 to 3 minutes on each side.
4. *Topping:* In microwave, heat the frozen fruit for 4-5 minutes.
5. Serve toasts immediately, and top them with the warm fruit and honey.

Bert's Egg-ly Cake

Makes four servings.

Ingredients
- 2 cups of vegetables (your choice), diced
- Salt and pepper to taste
- ¼ tablespoon of rosemary
- Cooking oil spray
- 3 whole eggs, beaten
- 1 egg white, beaten
- ¼ cup of fat-free milk

Procedure
1. Preheat oven to 350 degrees.
2. Sauté diced vegetables with salt, pepper, and rosemary in cooking oil spray in an ovenproof pan for 10-15 minutes. When veggies are soft, let them cool. Remember, use your favorite ones. I like to use tomatoes, stem-less spinach leaves, red bell pepper, mushrooms and cilantro. Play around and have fun!
3. Mix beaten eggs, egg white and milk. Pour the egg mixture onto the pan with the cooled-down, sautéed vegetables and stir together. Place in oven. Bake 15-20 minutes or until firm.
4. Enjoy!

Hashy-Hashies

Makes six to seven servings.

Ingredients
- Cooking oil spray
- 1 pkg. shredded potatoes
- 6 egg whites
- 2 whole eggs
- 1 teaspoon rosemary
- Salt to taste
- Optional: ½ cup of fat-free, shredded mozzarella cheese

Procedures
1. Preheat oven to 350 degrees. Spray cooking oil spray onto a baking pan (have it ready!)
2. Mix all ingredients and form into hand-sized patties.
3. Place the patties on the baking pan. Bake for 40 minutes or until golden brown on both sides; turn them over if necessary
4. Enjoy!

Snacks

Chip-a-Thon

Makes 2 servings.

Ingredients

- 12 (6-inch) round corn tortillas
- 2 tablespoons extra virgin olive oil
- 1 teaspoon salt
- 1 teaspoon of black pepper
- 1 teaspoon paprika

Tip: give the chips different flavor by using your favorite herbs and condiments

Procedure

1. Brush both sides of the tortillas with oil.
2. Make 2 stacks of six tortillas. Cut the stacks into 4 pieces.
3. Scatter chips, in a single layer, onto a large baking sheet.
4. Sprinkle them, evenly, with salt, pepper and paprika.
5. Bake 10 minutes. Flip chips over and bake for another 8-10 minutes until crispy and golden brown.

Hot Bert Faux-Fries

Makes two servings.

Ingredients

- Cooking oil spray
- 2 washed, unpeeled potatoes
- ½ tbsp. red pepper flakes
- ½ teaspoon chili powder
- Salt and pepper to taste
- Optional: 1 teaspoon paprika

Procedure

1. Preheat oven to 425 degrees. Spray baking pan with cooking oil spray (have it ready!)
2. Cut potatoes into wedges or strips. Place them in a mixing bowl and spray them three to four times with cooking oil spray.
3. Sprinkle with all spices and mix well.
4. Place potatoes on the pan in a single layer. Bake for 35-45 minutes or until they are a light brown color and crispy. Turn them over halfway through.
5. Enjoy!

Soups

Comfy Tomato Soup

Makes 2 servings.

Ingredients

- 2 small zucchini, coarsely chopped
- ½ carrot chopped
- ¼ cup chopped red onion
- ⅛ teaspoon salt
- 1 cup spicy hot V8 juice
- 1 small tomato cut into thin wedges
- 1 teaspoons canola oil
- ⅛ teaspoon dried thyme
- Pinch of black pepper
- 2-3 drops hot sauce (your choice) or pinch of chili powder

Procedure

1. In a large skillet, sauté zucchini, carrot, onion in canola oil tender, about 5-7 minutes. Sprinkle with salt.
2. Add the rest of ingredients; cook until heated through, serve immediately.

Bert's Green Cream

Makes four servings.

Ingredients

- 1 onion, chopped
- 1 zucchini, sliced
- 1 can of sweet peas, drained
- Cooking oil spray
- 3 cups of chicken broth
- 2 cups of spinach (baby spinach is best)
- 1 tbsp. of fresh cilantro, chopped
- 1 tbsp. of lemon juice
- Salt and parmesan cheese, for taste (optional)

Procedures

1. Place onion, zucchini and frozen peas in a saucepan coated with cooking spray. Sauté for 10-15 minutes or until zucchini is fully cooked.
2. Mix chicken broth with the sautéed vegetables and bring to a simmer. Add spinach, cilantro and lemon juice. Simmer for an extra five minutes.

3. Turn the stove off. Let the soup cool down for a while, then pour it into a food processor and blend until smooth. After blending, pour the soup back into a sauce pan and simmer for 5-10 additional minutes.
4. Optional: Before serving, sprinkle with salt and parmesan cheese.
5. Enjoy!

Hot Curry Chicken Corn Soup

Makes four servings.

Ingredients

- 2 skinless, boneless chicken breasts, pounded and diced
- ½ onion, chopped
- 3 tomatoes, diced
- 1 can of sweet corn, drained
- 3 tbsp. curry powder
- 1 tbsp. chili powder
- Optional: ½ tbsp. red pepper flakes
- 3 cups of chicken broth
- 1 potato, diced
- 1 ½ tbsp. salt or to taste

Procedure

1. Sauté chicken, onion, tomatoes and corn in a sauce pan with cooking spray for 10-15 minutes or until chicken is cooked.
2. Add curry and chili powder (and red pepper flakes, if desired) and mix well.
3. Add chicken broth, potatoes and salt. Simmer for 15-20 minutes or until potatoes are fully cooked.
4. Enjoy and savor!

Mamina's Cooing Butternut Soup

Makes 6 servings.

Ingredients

- 2 ripe pears, peeled, quartered and cored
- 2 pounds of butternut squash, peeled, seeded and cut into small chunks
- 2 medium tomatoes, cored and quartered
- 1 large leek, halved, sliced and washed
- 2 garlic cloves, crushed
- ½ teaspoon salt, divided
- 4 cups vegetable broth or reduced-sodium chicken broth, divided
- ⅔ cup of fat-free ricotta cheese
- 1 tablespoon fresh chives or greens scallion, sliced
- Freshly ground pepper to taste

Procedure

1. Preheat oven to 400°F.
2. Combine pears, squash, tomatoes, leek, garlic, salt and pepper in a large bowl; toss to coat. Spread evenly on a large baking sheet. Bake for 40-50 minutes or until vegetables are tender. Let the mix cool slightly.
3. Place vegetables and broth in a blender; puree until smooth. Puree, little by little, it will be easier and cleaner.
4. Add the smooth mixture to the pan and stir in the Ricotta Cheese.
5. Cook the soup over medium-low heat for an extra 10 minutes. Garnish with chives or green scallion.

Salads

Spin-A-Berry Salad

3-5 servings (it really doesn't matter; it's salad!)

Ingredients

- 2-3 cups (handfuls) of spinach leaves
- 1 cup of strawberries, rinsed and cut in four pieces
- 1 orange, peeled and cut in small pieces
- ¼ cup of raisins (or ¼ cup pecans)

Dressing #1
- ¼ cup of store-bought fat-free Italian dressing
- 1 tbsp. Dijon mustard
- ¼ cup raisins or pecans
- ¼ cup of 100% orange juice
- 1 tbsp. of vinegar
- Salt and pepper to taste

Dressing #2
- ½ fat-free plain yogurt
- ¼ teaspoon pepper
- 3 tablespoon Dijon mustard
- 3 tablespoon milk
- ½ teaspoon dried thyme
- 1 teaspoon 100% honey

Procedures

1. Mix the spinach, strawberries, orange pieces and raisins or pecans in a large mixing bowl
2. In a separate bowl, combine all the dressing ingredients and mix well.
3. Enjoy!

Orzo Summer Salad

Makes 4 servings.

Ingredients

- 1 cup orzo pasta
- ½ pound green beans
- 1 ½ tomatoes, chopped
- ¼ yellow pepper, chopped
- ½ onion, chopped
- 1 tablespoon parsley, chopped
- 1 tablespoon basil
- 1 teaspoon mint, chopped
- ½ cup roasted, lightly salted cashews or peanuts
- 1 tablespoon olive oil
- 1 tablespoon lemon juice and juice of ½ lemon, divided
- ¼ tablespoon pepper
- Salt to taste

Procedures

1. Cook the orzo in salted boiling water, drain and place on a baking sheet to cool. Drizzle juice of ½ lemon to prevent pasta from sticking.
2. Trim the green beans and cut in 1-inch pieces. Cook in boiling water for 4-5 minutes, then drain and plunge in cold water to stop cooking and set the vibrant green color.
3. Dressing: whisk olive oil, lemon juice, basil, parsley, mint, pepper and salt, together.
4. In a large bowl, mix the pasta, green beans, onion, tomatoes, yellow pepper, cashews and dressing. Let it cool. Serve.

Easy Rainbow Salad

Makes five servings.

Ingredients

- 2 cups of cooked whole wheat penne pasta
- 4 stalks of celery, coarsely chopped
- ½ onion, chopped
- 1 tbsp. of cilantro, chopped
- 2 tomatoes, diced
- 2 cans of tuna in water; drained
- 2 cups of fat-free plain yogurt
- Salt to taste

Procedure

1. Mix all ingredients well. Refrigerate before serving.

Entrees

Mac & Cheese, the Right Way

Makes five servings.

Ingredients

- 12 oz. cooked whole-wheat elbow macaroni pasta
- 2 cups butternut squash soup
- 1 cup fat-free milk or 1% milk or soy milk
- 1 cup part skim or reduced-fat mozzarella cheese, shredded
- 1 cup fat-free cheddar cheese or reduced-fat cheddar cheese, shredded
- 1 cup of parmesan cheese, shredded. It's best to use Parmigiano-Reggiano, the real stuff; it gives more freshness to the recipe.
- ½ onion, chopped
- Salt, to taste
- 1 teaspoon dried mustard
- ½ teaspoon of cayenne pepper
- ½ teaspoon of chili powder or Tabasco sauce or red pepper flakes
- Cooking oil spray

Topping:
- 3 tablespoons parmesan cheese, shredded
- 6 tablespoons unseasoned bread crumbs
- 1 teaspoon of plain fat free yogurt

Procedures

1. Preheat oven to 350 degrees.
2. In sauce pan, combine butternut squash soup puree, milk, mozzarella cheese, cheddar cheese, parmesan cheese and onion; cook over medium heat until melted. Turn off heat.
3. Add salt, dried mustard, cayenne pepper, and chili powder (or Tabasco or red pepper flakes—your choice).
4. Drain pasta; do not rinse. Combine it with cheese sauce and pour into shallow baking dish sprayed with cooking oil spray.
5. Topping: Mix parmesan cheese, bread crumbs and yogurt.
6. Sprinkle pasta with topping and bake for 15-20 minutes or until light brown.

Healthy Bert's Chili

Makes 8 servings.

Ingredients

- 1 lb. lean ground beef
- ½ cup chopped onion
- 3 cloves garlic, minced
- 1 (8 oz.) package of elbow macaroni, cooked
- ½ cup water
- 1 tbsp. chili powder
- 1 teaspoon dried mustard
- ½ teaspoon black pepper
- 1 can (14.5 oz) whole tomatoes; chopped—do not drain water
- 1 can of your choice of beans; drained—personally, I like red beans.
- 1 can whole kernel corn; drained
- 1 can (6 oz) tomato paste
- 1 (8 oz) can tomato sauce
- 1 cup fat-free cheddar cheese, shredded

Procedure

1. With cooking spray, cook beef, onion, pepper and garlic in a large pot. Drain well.
2. Return to pan, add macaroni and all other ingredients except cheese. Bring to boil. Then, reduce heat and simmer for 20 minutes.
3. Serve and sprinkle cheddar cheese to each portion.

Chicken Bert-lets

Makes four servings.

Ingredients

- Cooking oil spray
- 4 boneless, skinless chicken breasts
- ¼ cup chili powder
- 1 cup of Italian-style bread crumbs
- 1 cup of whole wheat flour
- 5 egg whites, beaten

Procedure

1. Preheat over 400 degrees. Spray baking pan with cooking spray (have it ready!).
2. Rinse and pound the chicken breasts for a more tender texture.
3. Mix chili powder with the Italian-style bread crumbs. Place the bread crumb mixture, whole wheat flour and egg whites in three separate containers.

4. Roll each chicken breast in whole wheat flour, then dip it in the beaten egg whites and then roll it in the bread crumb mix.
5. Place the chicken breast on the baking pan; bake for 25-30 minutes or until crisp.

Meatza Pizza

Makes 6-8 Servings

Ingredients
Dough
- 2 ½ cups whole wheat flour
- 1 package fast-acting dry yeast
- 1 teaspoon salt
- ⅔ cup cold water
- 1 teaspoon extra virgin olive oil
- ½ teaspoon 100% honey

Topping
- ⅓ pound ground beef
- ½ cup onion, chopped
- 1 clove garlic, minced
- 1 teaspoon chili powder
- ½ cup corn kernels
- ½ cup of mushrooms; sliced
- 3 tablespoons water
- ¼ teaspoon salt
- ½ teaspoon ground black pepper
- 2 tablespoons cilantro
- ½ cup fat-free or reduced fat cheddar cheese
- ½ cup fat-free or reduced fat mozzarella cheese

Procedure
Dough
1. Preheat oven to 425°C. Mix flour, yeast and salt, in large bowl. Mix water, oil and honey in another bowl.
2. Mix liquid mixture to the flour mixture, steadily. Mix well.
3. Roll the dough out on a non-stick, floured surface. Knead it vigorously for 5 minutes. Roll it up and put it in the refrigerator to cool.

Topping
4. In a saucepan, sprayed with cooking spray, cook the ground beef, onion, garlic, chili powder, corn kernels, mushrooms, water, salt, black pepper and cilantro. Cook until meat is brown.

Pizza

5. Unroll the pizza dough and put it on a, sprayed-with-cooking-spray, baking pan or pizza dish, pressing it down to make a thin crust. With your hands, give it the circular form.
6. Bake for about 5-8 minutes or until crust starts to turn golden brown.
7. Spread the ground beef mixture on the pizza crust. Sprinkle the pizza with the Cheddar and Mozzarella cheeses.
8. Bake pizza for 10 more minutes or until crust edges are golden brown and cheeses are melted.
9. Enjoy!

Creamy Spaghetti

Make 4 Servings.

Ingredients

- 1 (16 ounce) package of uncooked spaghetti
- ½ onion, chopped
- 1 tablespoon of garlic salt
- 1 tablespoon of fresh parsley, chopped
- 1 cup fat-free or 1% milk
- 1 cup fat-free or reduced fat mozzarella cheese
- 1 cup parmesan cheese
- 1 cup of mushrooms, sliced

Procedure

1. Bring a large pot of lightly salted water to a boil. Place spaghetti in the pot, cook for 8 to 10 minutes, until al dente, and drain.
2. Return to pot, sprayed with cooking oil spray, sauté, over low heat, the cooked pasta, onion, garlic salt and parsley, for 5-8 minutes.
3. Stir in milk, mushrooms and cheeses. Cook for another 5-8 minutes or until sauce turns thick.

Bert's Spicy Patties

Makes four servings.

Ingredients

- Cooking oil spray
- 1 pound of lean ground beef
- ½ cup of whole wheat flour
- 2 teaspoons baking powder
- 1 whole egg
- ½ onion, chopped

- 2 tomatoes, chopped
- 3 teaspoons red pepper flakes or jalapeños, diced
- Mozzarella cheese
- Salt

Procedure

1. Preheat oven 350 degrees. Spray baking pan with cooking oil spray (have it ready!)
2. Mix all ingredients well, except for the cheese.
3. Form mixture into round, hand-sized patties and place them in a baking pan.
4. Bake for 25-30 minutes; turn them over halfway through.
5. Serve sprinkled with cheese or eat between two whole wheat buns alongside, with some tomatoes and lettuce.

Desserts

Berry Melon Slushie

Makes 2 servings.

Ingredients

- 4 cups frozen seedless watermelon chunks
- 1 cup frozen strawberries
- 1-2 cups 100% orange juice
- OR 1 cup orange juice and 1 cup lemonade

Procedure

1. Freeze the watermelon and the strawberries (you can buy the already frozen berries, too!)
2. Add the watermelon and strawberries in a blender. Add the juice. Blend until smooth consistency is reached. Add more juice if necessary.
3. Serve.

Berry Bert's Crush

Ingredients

- 1 cup cherries; frozen and stoned
- 1 cup strawberries; frozen
- 1 cup raspberries; frozen
- 1 tablespoon brown sugar

Tip: have at least ¼ cup of water on the side; it might help to add just a little bit of water to the mix when blending.

Procedure

1. Put all ingredients in blender. Blend until really smooth.

Multi-Fruity Smoothie

Makes two to three servings.

Ingredients

- 1 banana, sliced
- 1 peach, diced
- 1 cup of blueberries, frozen
- 2 ½ cups fat-free milk
- 1 Dannon Light & Fit peach yogurt
- 1 ½ cups of ice

Procedure

1. Place all ingredients in a food processor and blend until smooth.
2. Sprinkle cinnamon on the top before serving.

Oatmeal A La Bert Cookies

Makes six or seven servings.

Ingredients

- 1 cup oat flour
- 1 cup rolled oats
- ½ cup unsweetened apple sauce
- ¾ cup Splenda or raw sugar
- ½ cup of raisins or pecans
- 1 egg
- ¼ cup fat-free milk
- ½ teaspoon baking soda
- 1 teaspoon of vanilla extract
- 1 pinch of salt
- Optional: 2 bananas, mashed

Procedure

1. Preheat oven 400 degrees.
2. In a large mixing bowl, combine all ingredients.

3. Using a tablespoon, make golf ball-size balls of dough. Place and press the dough balls onto a nonstick baking sheet. Remember to place them a few inches apart from each other.
4. Bake for 10-12 minutes or until brown (know your oven!).

Bert's BB Bread

Makes eight to ten servings.

Ingredients

- Cooking oil spray
- 1 cup of Splenda or raw sugar
- 1 tbsp. unsweetened apple sauce
- 2-3 ripe bananas, pureed
- 1 egg
- 1 teaspoon vanilla or coconut extract
- 1 cup oat flour or whole wheat flour
- ¾ teaspoon baking powder
- ½ teaspoon baking soda
- ¼ teaspoon salt
- ½ cup dried blueberries or raisins or pecans

Procedure

1. Preheat oven 350 degrees; spray cooking spray onto a loaf pan.
2. Mix all ingredients well in large mixing bowl. Pour mixture onto the pan. Bake 30 minutes or until a toothpick inserted comes out clean.
3. Delight in this delicious dessert!

Berry Cupcakes

Makes six to eight servings (one cupcake per serving).

Ingredients

- Cooking oil spray
- ¾ cup Splenda or raw sugar
- 1 cup (about 12-15) strawberries, pureed or crushed
- 2 tbsp. unsweetened apple sauce
- 1 teaspoon vanilla extract
- 2 egg whites, unbeaten
- 1 cup whole wheat flour or unbleached multi-purpose flour
- ½ teaspoon baking soda
- ¼ teaspoon salt

Frosting

(8 ounce) package fat-free cream cheese.
- ¼ cup powder sugar; this time, use Splenda, since it comes in a powdery texture
- ¼ teaspoon vanilla extract or strawberry extract
- 3 drops of red or green food coloring
- Frozen strawberries, halved

Procedure

1. Preheat oven to 350 degrees. Line cupcake pan with paper liners and spray them, once, with cooking spray.
2. On medium speed, beat together the first eight ingredients: sweetener, strawberries, apple sauce, vanilla extract, egg whites, flour, baking soda and salt.
3. Spoon batter into paper liners until ¾ is full. Bake for 20-25 minutes or until a wooden toothpick inserted in the middle of cupcakes comes out clean. Let them cool before frosting them.
4. Frosting: Blend together powdered milk, pinch of salt and Splenda. Once fully mixed, add the ¼ cup of plain yogurt and beat at low speed until mixture resembles fine crumbs. Add the remaining 2 tbsp. of yogurt and vanilla extract. Beat until thick consistency is reached. Chill before frosting cupcakes.
5. Enjoy this delightful treat!

Guilt-Free Faux Cheesecake

Makes eight servings.

Ingredients

Crust:
- Cooking oil spray
- 1 ½ cup graham crackers; crumbled
- 4 tbsp. unsweetened apple sauce
- 1 teaspoon cinnamon

Filling
- 4 cups fat-free cottage cheese or fat-free ricotta cheese
- ¾ cup Splenda or raw sugar
- 3 whole eggs
- 3 egg whites
- 1 teaspoon vanilla extract
- 1 tbsp. unsweetened apple sauce

Topping:
- 2 cups strawberries; diced
- ¼ cup milk

- 1 teaspoon vanilla extract
- 2 teaspoons Splenda

Procedure:

1. Preheat oven 350 degrees. Use a cheesecake pan with removable sides; spray pan with cooking oil.
2. Crust: Crush Graham crackers until fine. Mix apple sauce and cinnamon into the graham crackers; mix well. Pat the mixture into the bottom of the pan. Chill.
3. Filling: Blend cottage cheese in food processor until smooth (process bit by bit; it's easier). Place cottage cheese mixture in a large mixing bowl and add the sugar, whole eggs, egg whites, vanilla extract and unsweetened apple sauce. Mix well.
4. Pour filling mixture over the chilled crust. Cover with foil and bake for 60 minutes or until a wooden toothpick inserted in the center comes out clean. Afterwards, chill for at least 45-60 minutes.
5. Topping: Spray a small sauce pan with cooking oil spray. Mix strawberries, milk, vanilla extract and Splenda; simmer over medium heat for 5-10 minutes. Remove from heat and let cool for a few minutes; then put the mixture in a food processor and blend until smooth. Chill completely before pouring over cheesecake.
6. Enjoy!

Chapter 21

Just to Point It Out, I Love Myself
Present Time

To love oneself is the beginning of a lifelong romance.
—Oscar Wilde

AFTER THE PROGRAM ENDED, EVERYONE AROUND ME—MYSELF included—was worried that I was going to fall back again into the obesity hole by going back to my old ways and finally entering the dark Diabetic Zone without the coaching from Cindy and Thea and weekly check-ups, I felt kind of alone as if I had nobody to protect me. Certainly I had my parents, but I didn't have anyone like Cindy and Thea.

I remember voicing my doubts to my mom. We were having dinner, and I realized she had some doubts, too. I turned to my dad, looking for a different response. My dad is a man of few words—*very, very* few words. But this time, he broke out, surprisingly. He merely turned to me and connected with my eyes. With a very somber facial expression, he told me, "Stop! It's all gonna be fine. Don't let your fears dictate what's going to happen. You'll be fine. You know what to do."

Immediately, my mom turned to me and grabbed my hand. "That's true. We have been, and will still be, here for you, right beside you. We all have the tools that Cindy and Thea gave us. So if you forget one, I'll remind you, and if I forget one, you'll remind me. And we have your dad as back-up . . . somewhat."

She giggled and then continued. "Also, remember, we are pros at using the tools now. This is going to be an easy ride, because this is not a diet! This is . . ."

I interrupted, my eyes looking straight into hers. As if it were a meditation mantra, we both said at the same time, "A new, healthy lifestyle."

My dad chuckled, my mom smiled and my heart and mind were put at ease as we continued eating.

Everything they had said was spot on. Naturally, I was afraid—who wouldn't be? I had been fighting against obesity for what seemed like my entire life. I knew its power and strength and I also knew I had a history of quitting. But this time was going to be different. I wasn't going to give up all the hard work and time I had put into changing my life just because I was scared.

The days, months and years began to pass by. Today, I'm sitting here sharing my story with you! I still struggle some days. Other days are a stroll in the park. On days when I am too busy to go to the gym, I practice yoga at home. Other days, I eat two more Red Light Foods than usual (my limit is ten per week). But some days, I only eat one Red Light Food, and some days, zero Reds. I have made some missteps, once in a while; by no means am I saying I became perfect after the program. It's hard work to maintain and continue rebuilding a new life. I have to work at it daily. I have to embrace it, indulge it, take care of it and give my new life a pat on the back now and then. It has become a bit demanding, but it's my life. If I don't care about myself, who will? It's good to take care of oneself. Love yourself. Respect yourself. Worry about yourself. Your self is the only true thing you have until you die. Why not take care of it and enjoy it, in the meantime?

What do I eat? I eat every single type of food you can imagine, from poultry to meat to fish to shellfish to tofu to vegetables to fruits to rice cakes to pretzels to Guilt-Free Faux Cheesecake. Of course, there are some Red Light Foods I choose not to eat or at least try to avoid, since I know how damaging they are to my body. In other words, I do pay attention to what I put into my mouth. I don't want to put crappy, greasy food into my mouth that will affect me later on.

Today, the tools have become an important part of my life. They are no longer part of a weight-control program; instead, they are my life. I use the tools to build a new life.

The new changes led me to shed thirty pounds during the program, the healthy way. In the new lifestyle I developed I was able to lose a few more pounds. I've lost an extra forty pounds! Thanks to my new way of living, I've lost a total of sixty-nine pounds.

I went from weighing as much as a newborn elephant to weighing what a normal teen should weigh. The best part of all is that I've managed to keep those pounds off, since I lost them in a very healthy manner. I didn't lose them through starving myself to death or working out 24/7 or puking my guts out. I haven't regained the weight, because this is not a diet. I don't exercise excessively, because a diet is not telling me or my parents that I need to do that. I feel full of energy, more agile and I'm able to run a mile. I'm not skin and bones. I do have a bit of meat, but I am healthy and I look good. I eat all the foods I love and enjoy. And no diet would have gotten me here.

Have I changed? Obviously. If you see me now and you saw me then, you'd know I've changed physically. I moved from XL shirts to Small. I revolutionized the size of my jeans, going from a 38-inch waist to a 30. I no longer have to share my underwear with my dad, because his don't fit me anymore. I no longer have to buy huge, yellow raincoats to hide myself, baggy shorts to hide my turkey legs or huge sweaters to cover up my bulge. I don't have to wear yellow or orange Hawaiian shirts at the beach or at the pool anymore. I am no longer afraid of taking my T-shirt off. Now, I love taking my shirt off. I want to show off my new look. Who wouldn't?

My perception of food has changed. Food is food now, and my life is my life. I have control over food and I don't let it run the show anymore. The way I live and see life certainly has changed. The way I respect and love myself has absolutely changed. And the way I think about exercise and television has undergone a remarkable change.

A big part of me has changed for the better, but I'm still the same person on the inside: the same respectful, down-to-earth, loving, slightly demanding kid still lives within me. I am a healthier version of Curly (and better looking, too!), and I'm still trying to be funny and dorky. I'm not the "fat ass geek" or the class clown anymore, but I still love science, math, art, social studies. I may not look like El Gordito anymore, but on the inside, I'm still El Gordito. My mom still calls me that from time to time, even though I don't look anything like it. But I don't mind, since the new Gordito is a better version of the old one.

I'm still shy, although not as much as I was before. This transformation has given a tremendous boost to my self-confidence and self-esteem. Looking the way I once envisioned myself —the way I'm supposed to look—makes me feel like a part of the rest of the world. And, most of all, I'm happy! I don't feel like an alien or the weirdo kid that everybody points at, who sits at the back of the classroom pretending he doesn't exist.

Now I have a bit more confidence to go up to people, to be part of a group, to raise my hand whenever I have a question, to give my opinion, to speak up, to laugh, to make a fool out of myself. I'm not so nervous anymore about someone looking at me. I know they're not looking at my over-the-waistband bulge or my stretch marks or my forty-year-old man boobs. Now I can go out there and present myself to the world, the way I was supposed to be all along. I'm not embarrassed about the way I look, anymore. I love myself. I enjoy myself. I love being the way I am.

Bert is my best friend. And I am Bert's best friend.